Decisions of Change:
The Choice Is Yours

Kenneth L. Meadors

My Journey Back to Father's House

Contents

A FOREWORD BY KEN'S FATHER

As the father of Kenneth Larry Meadors, I have a close-up view of the wonderful work that is taking place in his life. My wife, Nancy, and I have been dedicated to the service of the Lord from a young age and have been actively involved in ministry together for fifty-seven years now. As the son of a pastor, I am sure that Kenny has felt like he has lived in a glass house with expectations that were overwhelming at times. Yet, through all of his struggles in life, he has always had a strong faith in God, and for this we rejoice and give God the glory.

I will seek to give witness to a miraculous story of recovery and restoration by presenting some background information on Kenny's life that will verify the goodness of God. I believe that you as well as I will certainly see that the calling of God is certain and will be fulfilled, not only in Kenny's life, but all who have a calling upon their life. Make no mistake about it, everyone has a calling on their life, even though they may not see or understand it yet. All may not necessarily be preachers, but all have a ministry to fulfill in manifesting the grace of God to a hurting generation.

God has kept His mighty hand on Kenny through numerous events in his life. He is a true miracle to still be in the land of the living. There is no doubt in my mind that God has preserved Kenny for such a time as this to be a voice of mercy and grace to a generation that desperately needs it. I will never forget the telephone call that I received on a Saturday morning, June 9, 1979, when Kenny was fifteen years old. It was from a hospital in Poplar Bluff, Missouri informing me that our son had been in an accident. When I inquired concerning the other passengers, I was told to call the Highway Patrol. I knew that something tragic had happened. I was told the devastating news that four members of my family were killed in the accident. Kenny survived, even though he had gotten some serious injuries.

I could relate many, many other incidents where the mercy of God was extended to Kenny. I had heard him state that he didn't deserve to survive the accident that took the lives of his Maw Maw and Paw Paw. That began a downward spiral that lasted until this past August of the year 2016 when Kenny began his upward climb back to sobriety and fulfillment of purpose. I and my wife Nancy can testify that drug addiction and alcoholism affects the whole family, and we have prayed many prayers for the salvation of our children and that they find their full purpose in life. We know that God had a divine plan for Kenny, but it seemed that we would never see the fulfillment of it. But, thanks be unto God, we have reason to rejoice as we see the work of restoration taking place in the life of our son.

Kenny was always a hard worker who was very accomplished in many areas, including carpentry and painting. He rarely missed work because of his addictions, but he deprived his family of the support they needed in order to support his addictions. His failures has led to guilt and shame that has been overwhelming. He deals with these issues in this book and has shown that there is complete healing in the Lord Jesus Christ.

I know that there are no doubt many who have or are experiencing the same problems that Kenny has experienced, and I believe that his experiences will be a great inspiration to help others to find restoration to their God as well as to their families. Kenny is presently a part of the discipleship program at the Center of Hope in Anniston, Alabama, and he is already involved in the ministry of helping other members of the program—especially the younger men who are struggling with the same problems as Kenny. I believe he will be a tremendous asset to the Kingdom of God in the remaining years of his life here on earth.

I can testify that Kenny has always had a heart for God even in his darkest hours. Although he may have questioned God on many occasions, as far as I know, he has always had a strong faith in God. He has told me on many occasions that he of all four of our children would be the one to take up my mantle as a minister of the gospel. Of course there were times I couldn't see this, but now I have no doubt. I am astound at his understanding of the Word of God, especially as it relates to what I consider to be "present truth." He also has a very effective delivery of that Word. In fact, I am absolutely amazed at his writing of this book. The book is his story told as only Kenny can communicate.

I pray that Kenny will continue to utilize the experiences he has gone through to relate to others who need to be delivered from their bondage to addictions. Even though he has been in numerous rehab programs, I now see something of a miraculous nature that has occurred in his life. He has been completely focused on fulfilling his God-given purpose, and I am thrilled and excited to see what is yet in store for his life.

As my daughter has expressed to me, this book can be beneficial to anyone who reads it even though they may not be experiencing addictions to drugs and alcohol. This is true because what Kenny is communicating can relate to any life situation that people are dealing with. What is interesting is how he has interwoven his own experiences with biblical characters with whom he has identified. My prayer is that many will be positively affected after having read this book.

I believe that I and my wife will see the restoration of a loving relationship of Kenny with his children and grandchildren. Even though his problems have affected his relationship with his present wife Kimberly, there is an eternal bond that will be strengthened. I want to thank Kimberly for her stand and support of Kenny in helping him come to grips with his life problems. The wonderful part of this whole process is that Kenny is not doing what he is doing for anyone or for any other reason than to experience freedom and to see his calling and purpose fulfilled.

I know that if God can do a miraculous work in our son, then he can and will do the same for anyone who trusts Him. May God's blessings be upon all who are struggling with personal problems that have held them in debilitating captivity from which they seek liberation. God is a good God, who is full of mercy and grace, and will meet us at our point of need. May the Lord Jesus Christ be revealed to you in a supernatural manner that will change your life forever and will allow you to live your life more abundantly.

Dr. W. Kenneth Meadors

DEDICATION

"What are you willing to do to change?" These were the very words that were spoken to me as I walked into my first Alcoholic Anonymous (AA) meeting at Three Rivers Mental Health Facility in Cedartown, Georgia. I was admitted into their drug/alcohol abuse program about fifteen years ago. As I entered the room, my eyes became affixed to a black man in a blue suit, and for the first time in years, I heard the voice of God speak to me, "Do you see that man?" My thoughts were, "How could I not see him?" God spoke again saying, "I'm putting him in your life for the rest of your life." Not to get into detail, he remains in my life to this day as my friend and mentor.

Briefly as I can be, let me say that my initial meeting with this man was not a direct connection. In fact, I left the meeting in anger when he told me I needed to go back out and get high. He spoke these words after I refused to remove my billfold from one pocket and place it in another pocket. In anger I said, "What the hell does that have to do with recovery?" He told me that recovery was about *change,* and *change* requires following directions. He stated that if I couldn't follow a simple instruction to remove my billfold from one pocket to another pocket, then I sure couldn't change my life.

As I turned and began to walk away, he spoke and said, "Hey, mad about it? When you get ready to go to bed tonight, take your shoes off and throw them under your bed." I turned and walked back to the table where he sat and leaned down and said, "What does that have to do with change? His blunt voice said, "You will figure it out in the morning."

As he placed his things in his briefcase and walked away, out of curiosity, I did what he requested and placed my shoes way under the bed that night. The next morning as I was slinging choice words around the room for having to literally get down on both knees and reach under my bed, then it hit me. I was in a praying position. I asked God to help me as I wept. I reached into my back left pocket to remove my billfold and placed it into my back right pocket where it remains. This man's name is Pastor Ahue Sims. To this man, I owe my life.

Change began that morning and continues until this day. I dedicate this book to you, Sims. Without you, I would have given up a long time ago. Without your continued support in my life, I would not have lived to tell my story. God has held true to His Word, and you have remained in my life. For those who know him, know his heart. For those who don't, let me say, "He knows how to get the smell of the street on him as he still at the age of 73 returns weekly to the streets of Atlanta, Georgia to share the love of Jesus to the homeless people that he once lived with."

Sims and I both have had moments of relapse—moments of frustration. Things are not always peaches and cream. Actually, there are times that they just plain suck! Sims and I have experienced loss of family and friends. I received news of two more of my friends who have passed just this week. We both have experienced divorce and even incarceration, yet we keep going. It was the choice we made, and a promise we have to each other. We chose to never give up, and we promised each other to always help those who are less fortunate.

It is because of this choice that I live to tell my story. When asked the question why, I simply say, "The spirit of the Lord is upon me, because He has anointed me to preach good news to the poor; he has sent me to proclaim freedom for the prisoners and recovery to the blind, to release the oppressed, to proclaim the year of the Lord's favor!" (Luke 4:18-19, New International Version of the Bible).

Special Acknowledgments

Bishop Darrell Gooden, you will always remain my pastor. Not many understand your simplicity and "country boy" ways. Yet, it took both to relate to me, and I thank God for you being in my life. I may not talk to you daily or even monthly, but I know that when I need you, you will always be there. I love you and Kathy with all my heart.

To the late Bishop David Huskins—I watched from the sidelines as I witnessed your change from a young boy to become a bishop. Your life alone was words enough.

Dr. Lynn Hiles, your dynamic preaching style and the power of the message of grace that you preach has forever changed my life. When I was hungry, you fed me. May the words of this book reflect the impact you have had in my world of change. I am forever grateful.

Dr. Kenneth Meadors (Dad), there is none like you. You have stood the test of time. It is an honor to be your first-born son, and it is my privilege to carry the torch unto another generation.

These four men have had a hands-on impact in the molding of who I am today. Scripture tells us to not call anyone on earth Father. However, it honors me to call Dr. Kenneth Meadors my father—both spiritually and naturally. He has had an impact on many ministers of today. He was the Dean of Academic Affairs of Vineyard Harvester Bible College, and his teaching has been viewed on a global level. Join me as I salute this man of God who I refer to as *Pastor Dad*.

I want to thank my Dad, Dr. Kenneth Meadors and my uncle, Dr. Ray Meadors for their help in proofreading and editing.

INTRODUCTION

As I sit in silence in the Day Room of Center of Hope (COH), waiting on God to speak to me, I read the words "Decisions, Decisions" that graced the face of a Coca-Cola machine. I smiled, then laughed momentarily as I realized God had spoken to me from a Coca-Cola machine! I laughed as Coca-Cola was once the topic of sin that was often preached from the pulpits of "terroristic preachers." They would pull their pants up halfway across their large bellies and start naming sin. Coca-Cola was a sin to drink because the shape of the bottle would create a lust for a woman. I guess it was only a sin for men. Dr. Lynn Hiles says it best, "If Coca-Cola causes you to lust, buy a 3-liter and get over it!" Our daily lives are full of decisions, and with each decision we make creates within itself a need for change. On this same Coca-Cola machine, it also read, "Make a choice and enjoy." It was clearly the voice of God.

I smiled, then laughed momentarily as I realized God had spoken to me from a Coca-Cola machine!

Center of Hope (COH) is a discipleship program in Anniston, Alabama. It is without question the greatest outreach ministry that I have ever been affiliated with. I recommend and encourage all who read this book to learn of its existence, its purpose, and to get connected with the ministry that flows from it.

The main focus of COH is the streets, and its purpose is to bring the unwanted, the afflicted, the drug addicted, and drug dealer to a change of direction for their lives. It provides a place where the alcoholic, the pimp, or the prostitute have a place of refuge where they are taught of a loving God who loves them and is not "out to get them." COH is unlike most places, such as Rehabs (as well as churches), that limit their outreach only to salvation with a congratulation followed by a handshake and a smile.

The Center of Hope teaches the new convert how to become committed, responsible, and accountable disciples of Jesus Christ. They offer a twelve to eighteen-month discipleship program that includes parenting classes, but my favorite is the Authentic Manhood classes. Throughout this extended program, they teach the new converts to walk and grow into true disciples of a living God.

I stand in amazement every Sunday morning and Wednesday night as hundreds of men and women flood the altars to worship—men and women who have been rescued from the streets praying for one another. They lift their hands in praise to a God they once thought was an angry God who was out to get them. Talking about change—they lift up arms that have more tattoos than hair; and, arms that have bullet wounds and scars that are physical trademarks of the streets that they once roamed. These arms that were once used as weapons are now used for worship. Without question, these represent a demonstration of visible mercy and grace.

I have always said that the real preachers are in the streets, because the traditional church has not offered them hope. The church should be a place of refuge and rest. Most of all, someone forgot to tell people who they are. They have all, including me, made bad decisions in life, and we all have paid dearly as we have dealt with the consequences of our bad decisions.

Romans 3:21-24 (NIV) explains it best:

"But now apart from the law the righteousness of God has been made known, to which the Law and the Prophets testify. This righteousness is given through faith in[a] Jesus Christ to all who believe. There is no difference between Jew and Gentile, for all have sinned and fall short of the glory of God, and all are justified freely by his grace through the redemption that came by Christ Jesus."

Our redemption is a done deal. We can do nothing of ourselves to receive such grace. We only qualify ourselves for this grace by the scars on our hearts and the stench of our clothes that reek with the smell of the streets that we lived in. We need no other recommendations, especially from religious-minded people whose only motive is to "sin search" our lives.

No Recommendation Needed

A famous doctor, who was known for his kindness, met a dirty, ragged boy on the street. The boy boldly asked to be taken into the doctor's home. The doctor said, "I know nothing of you, my boy. What do you have to recommend yourself?" The little boy pointed to his ragged clothes and said, "I thought these would be enough." The doctor gathered him into his arms and took him home with him.

Everything that Jesus taught about our Father offers this same hope. We have nothing to recommend us but our hunger, weakness, and ragged clothes. And, these are enough. We are the closest to God's compassion when we are the weakest and most vulnerable. We can't claim anything to ourselves—no goodness, no intelligence, no beauty, no great work in any way that can recommend us to God. Only our desperate need for help provides our letter of recommendation.

It is our pain and our need that impresses God. When we ask, He gathers us up into His arms and takes us home. As we present our powerlessness and unmanageable lives to God, we get God's attention. Jesus came to heal the sick and suffering. He came for the least and the lost. He came for us. He came in our weakness and need, not in our strength and self-sufficiency.

Join me now through the pages of this book as I share my own life stories along with biblical characters to show the necessity of change. True change is an exchange. It's an exchange of your life for the life of Christ Jesus. The choice is yours, yet the question is, "What are you willing to do to experience a permanent change in your personal life?"

Chapter One

RECOGNIZING A NEED FOR CHANGE

Here I am once again with pen in hand as I sit in "quiet time" here at the Center of Hope. Quiet time is a one-hour period that is required of everyone in the discipleship program to spend time with God. It is when we study our Bibles or other related materials. It is my Hour of Power. Tonight, I had chosen to reflect over my Authentic Manhood workbook. As I may have previously stated, it's my favorite class and subject of study. I have always desired to be a good man (productive) but seemed to have always fallen short. In my workbook, I stumbled across the word *grief*. It took my full attention as grieving is what I have been doing all my life. I knew it was time for a change, and I couldn't think of any better place to start than by dealing with past losses and my inability to deal with them properly.

Like I said, grieving is what I had been doing for the majority of my life from being molested by another man at the age of five to losing four members of my immediate family in a costly major automobile accident when I was fifteen years old. I was one of only two survivors of that accident. Then, at the tender young age of eighteen, I was married to a young woman who owned my heart, only to find out that she was unfaithful to me. Although I had already been drinking and using some drugs, this event alone created a drug and alcohol dependency that would fuel a destructive lifestyle for the next thirty-four years of my life.

In addition to the previously mentioned incidents, I have survived multiple automobile accidents. One accident claimed yet another life as an 82-year old lady died in my arms as she begged me to not let her die. I could write a book just on this event alone. I have survived multiple drug overdoses, both intentional and non-intentional. I have survived blood alcohol levels of over .50 on several occasions. Additionally, I have suffered heart failure, diabetic coma (twice), and *necrotizing fasciitis* in my neck and throat. The surgeon told my father that if I had waited another six hours to get to the hospital, they would have been coming to my funeral. This is to only name a few.

Through the years, I have experienced loss, after loss, after loss, and the trauma of loss continues until this day. I have been separated from my children and grandchildren from the effects of not properly dealing with grief. The process of grieving creates a need for change. Actually, it is a process of change within itself. Grieving is exhaustive and leaves one as an open throat of depression. Depression that is not dealt with properly can and will lead to suicidal tendencies. Through such change, we must realize that there are times that we need to be gentle with ourselves. If we are not, we will become victims of self-guilt, shame, and most of all, self-condemnation.

My present wife is my fourth, and she no longer lives with me. Devastated once again, I ran back to what I knew best—grieving. Grieving is grieving—I don't care how you look at it. Yet, there are times that people such as myself who have just plain out disguised our *feel sorry for me* attitudes with the appearance of grieving. This is a deception, and I will speak of deception in a later chapter.

As you can see, the trauma of loss affected every area of my life. I would experience times of sobriety that lasted only long enough to make empty promises to my children, to my parents, to the Church, to my wife, and to myself. Un-dealt-with grief was the cause of my depression. I became a *pretender* as I began pretending as nothing was wrong. I lived behind a lie that said, "I'm okay," when in actuality, I had fallen apart. I will also address pretending in more detail in a later chapter.

Grief is a result of a broken heart. I first recognized my brokenness during a time that I was in a Teen Challenge Program in Milford, Ohio. It was there that I got the words of my poem, *The Sound of a Broken Heart.* Following is a short form of that poem:

The heart, like a crystal vase that sits upon a table top;
Seemingly stable and secure, until it is shaken to the table's
edge...where it drops.
The sound of the fall is silent and goes unheard,
Till the sound of shattered glass that dances across the
floor.
Now the childhood of Humpty Dumpty has become a
reality,
As my heart, like Humpty Dumpty, can't be put back
together again.

I was a wounded man and had no idea how wounded I was
until I became suicidal in thought. Not willing to put a gun to my
head, I would turn to suicidal levels of drug and alcohol use. I
began using lethal doses by method of Intravenous (IV) use. Once
again, I would cry out for help from God to heal me or kill me!

Another shorten version of a poem I wrote:

"Voices"

The voices that continue to sing inside my head
Are the voices of hell's angels chanting for my death.
I know that I am only to blame, but how do they know me
by my name?
Why do they tell me..."stick the needle in your vein?"
Oh Lord, is this the one? Or do I live to only fix another one?
If I do, then please take my life.
I can no longer control that which is inside.

I had now become enslaved by self-shame, self-blame,
guilt, and the grandfather of them all—self-condemnation. The
weight of their presence was more than I could bear and always
caused a need for self-medication. Drugs and alcohol are only
temporary solutions to a permanent problem. Actually, it's not

even a solution at all. The truth is, you can't find even a temporary solution to any spiritual problem by natural means.

Drugs and alcohol are only temporary solutions to a permanent problem.

The first process of change is the realization of a need for it. No change can take place without the loss of something else. For me, an old lifestyle had to die. Old ideals and thoughts of who I was had to die. Change takes courage, as courage activates all other virtues in life. I pray that by the time you finish reading this book, you will become encouraged to change.

I think I have now established the fact that loss (of any kind) creates a process of grieving. As tragic as it can be, and has been in my life, grieving can be good and aid in the process of change. Grieving is a healthy emotion that God has given us. It is designed to bring closure to the tragedies of our lives. Unattended, grief is heavy and destructive, not only to the griever, but also to those whose lives are connected to them. It causes weariness and will deplete our ability to function in other areas of our lives. It causes isolation and desolation to the point that loneliness is our only friend.

Loneliness gives birth to self-centeredness as it did in my own life. We become so self-centered that nothing else matters to us—not even our own children. My heart gets heavy every time I think of the damages that I have caused in the lives of my own children because of my self-centered and selfish lifestyle. The heaviness of grief that had become fueled by the consciousness of my wrongs gave birth to self-guilt, self-shame, and self-blame, all of which are children of self-condemnation.

The first process of change is the realization of a need for it.

It was here that I had become suicidal. I had lost the will to live. Not only have I experienced the outcome of unmanaged grief, I now have witnessed its subtle approach as it has weaved itself to my brothers and my mother. I see it trying to attach itself to my father, but it has not yet prevailed. It is only by the grace of a living God that I live to pen my thoughts and discoveries of the life-threatening attack of the enemy. Grief causes loneliness and isolation. Our isolations are also deceiving, and at times, unidentifiable from our own inward perspective. It is a chameleon in nature as it blends into our daily lives.

I, as well as my youngest brother, Lyle Copeland Meadors, were more transparent in our lives, and our self-diagnoses were plainly seen in our outward lives that were controlled by drugs. However, my other brother, Brandon Raymond Meadors and my mother, Nancy "Nanny" Meadors were more closed-faced to the chokehold of grief. Brandon was very reclusive and solitary all his life, and became extremely so after the tragic death of his wife. Brandon has now gone to be with "the love of his life," and Lyle has likewise joined him in heaven. My heart was once again shattered to pieces. I write this chapter in memory of them both. I know they help me now as I have to reach deep into myself and deal with a life-long series of grief. I pray that in doing so, that my life's issues can bring healing to someone who has found themselves in the chokehold of grief. Grief is good when properly dealt with. It is designed to heal, not to kill.

I did not realize that grief was good. I only perceived it as an enemy or a consequence of my wrong. The misunderstanding of the principle of "sowing and reaping" caused me to only think that I was getting what I deserved. My perspective was what needed change. These are the old ideas and thoughts that had become the principalities and powers in my life. Principalities are nothing more than distorted principles.

I am reminded of Abraham's faith in God to fulfill his promise to him. Abraham refused to consider anything other than God's promise to him. To consider something is to fix your eyes upon it. My question to you now is, "What are you focused on? Is it your circumstances or your solution?" A title to a book that was written by my uncle, Dr. Ray E. Meadors, was *Solution-focused Marriage*. Solution-focused is what we must do in order to achieve change in whatever dilemma we are facing. Even the Apostle Paul stated, "We become changed by simply fixing our eyes (focusing) on our solution." That solution is the Word of God.

My perspective of myself had to change. Just a couple of days ago, as I was walking in the cool, dark morning hour from the dormitory rooms of Center of Hope to the mess hall to begin breakfast for the students, I asked God to help me see myself as He sees me. Later that morning a fellow student came to me and stated how something had come over him, and he had no explanation for why he was feeling so full of compassion. As he began to explain his feelings, he began to weep. I felt a spiritual presence overtake me. As he began to speak, I closed my eyes and these are the words he spoke:

> "When I first looked into my new born son's face, I became speechless for words; I couldn't take my eyes off him as I held him in my arms. The more I looked into his eyes, I saw the reflection of myself. What I saw was all that I am. I realized that he was the exact nature of myself."

As my eyes immediately opened, I shouted so loud that he about jumped out of his jeans! I asked if he would repeat himself, and I explained why. God answered my request through an audible voice. His answer was one of compassion and love, not anger and vengeance. God did not see the wrongs in my life, nor did He mention anything of seeing any sin. All he saw was "His son," and in this son (me), he saw his own nature. No longer do I reflect the nature of the dead (Adam), but I now reflect the nature of a "son." It amazes me to see how many people who confess to be children of God still remain in bondage to "self."

Satan does not have the authority to put you in bondage. All he can do is run his big, big mouth that shouts out accusations against the Word of God. To be solution-focused is what I refer to as the simplicity of the Gospel. Simplicity is by definition, to be single focused. Single focused on Jesus Christ and His finished work of redemption will in fact bring you into a "resting place." As I may have mentioned previously and will continue to repeat myself throughout the remaining chapters of this book, my change is effortless and is shown in my life as I now live life with an *unforced rhythm of grace.*

Satan does not have the authority to put you in bondage. All he can do is run his big, big mouth that shouts out accusations against the Word of God.

Chapter Two

DEALING WITH GRIEF

As I began my process of change by recognizing my problem of grief, I knew that I could no longer sweep it under the rug and pretend as it did not exist. I had to deal with this ever-existing problem that had controlled my entire life. I began meditating, and in prayer, I asked God for understanding. As I began re-thinking past events, my emotions began to re-surface. Referring to the Book of James, quoting from the New Living Translation (NLT) version of the Bible—James 1:2-3:

> "Dear brothers and sisters, when troubles of any kind comes your way *(notice that James states that trouble will come your way, not if it comes your way)*, consider it an opportunity for great joy. For you know that when your faith is tested, your endurance has a chance to grow."

This gives proof that we can and will profit from our times of trouble. James is telling us that we can learn and grow through our troublesome times. The story of Job does just that! It gives us a beautiful illustration of the redemptive work of Calvary's Hill. It's all about restoration and healing; it's about perseverance, patience, and being steadfast. We can't know the depth of our character until we see how we react under pressure.

I once stated jokingly that I was built for battle because when it gets too tough for everyone else, it's just right for me. Follow me now as I journey back through some of my life's lessons that parallel the life of Job. The study of Job is an ancient story of a righteous man that had done no wrong and did not deserve the tragedy of losses he experienced. The story gives an answer to the often asked question, "Why do bad things happen to good people?"

We can't know the depth of our character until we see how we react under pressure.

Job, like myself, spent countless hours in vain attempts to identify the reason for the hell he was experiencing. Unlike Job, who kept his faith in God and maintained his innocence, I fell apart at the seams. Job was innocent—I wasn't. Job kept his faith—I let go of my faith. Yet, one common thing returned; we both experienced the devastating effects of unmanaged grief.

My grief caused me to become naked and ashamed much like that of the Genesis account of Adam and Eve. I, like Adam, turned to the self-help method of covering up. The only difference was Adam began sewing leaves, and I began smoking weed.

In Job 3:11, we find where Job had three friends who came to help him. As they journeyed to their friend, I would imagine that they discussed their fool-proof plan to help deliver their friend from his agony. Upon their arrival, they saw the condition of their friend. In complete devastation, they began ripping their clothes and crying. I don't think their cries were a tear or two. I believe they were mourning as if someone had passed away.

I will never forget the time that I received the phone call from my Dad with the news of the death of my brother, Brandon. I was sitting in the passenger side of my boss's truck when my phone began to ring. When I answered, I knew something was wrong. I first thought it was news of my other brother, Lyle. I would have expected it to have been him. When I asked my Dad if it was Lyle, he said, "No, it's Brandon." I opened the door of the truck and fell to the ground screaming, "No! No! Oh, God, no!" My heart was again shattered as I lay face down on the ground gripping handfuls of grass and crying to the point that I began vomiting.

This is how I also see Job's friends. Scripture tells how these friends remained speechless for the next seven days. I was no different! I could not even go into the small country store to even buy a pack of cigarettes. All I could do was point to what I wanted. Everyone around me was also speechless. They wanted to speak to me but knew not what to say that would comfort me in my condition. What they did not realize was just their silence was comfort enough. As days passed, and I traveled to Georgia to attend my brother funeral, I continued to weep uncontrollably. In Job's situation, his friends' presence was enough. Their greatest support was found in their silence. I can relate to the comfort that Job must have experienced, just knowing they were there for him.

I have also been through very traumatic times of detoxing off of drugs and alcohol where fear of death would overtake me. The presence of death was real and tangible to all who were present in the house. Tears would fill their eyes as their prayers would become loud as thunder. I weep now as my thoughts take me back to those moments of my life. In those moments of suffering, moments of unconsciousness would rise an inability to respond to my mother's voice as she herself would cry out in mourning, shouting, "We have lost him! Oh, God help us. We have lost him!" My body turned cold; my skin was a pale white, and my breathing had stopped momentarily as my father was driving frantically, rushing me to the nearest emergency room. In fact, my mother and I were exchanging our last good-byes.

On another occasion, I will never forget the look on my oldest daughter's face as her eyes were filled with tear drops like ponds of soft-fallen dew. Tear drops rolled down her cheeks like two leaking faucets as they carried me out of her home on a stretcher. "Don't give up, Daddy," she would say to me as I pleaded with the EMS team to please let me die. Through those times of detoxing, it would bring me comfort just knowing someone was present with me.

Grief had a choke hold on me, and I had become as Job in chapter 3, verses 1-3, and I quote:

"After this, Job opened his mouth and cursed the day of his birth. He said, 'May the day of my birth perish, and the night it was said, 'a boy is born.'" (NIV)

In verse 8 of chapter three, it also states:

"May those who curse days curse that day, those who are ready to rouse Leviathan."

Leviathan, or the spirit of leviathan, is nothing less than the devil himself and the spirit of death. Those who rouse this spirit are those who were in my circle of drug use that manufactured methamphetamines. Meth is nothing more than the devil himself in a materialistic form. The manufacturing of the drug is modern-day sorcery. This is all I will say concerning this Leviathan spirit.

Meth is nothing more than the devil himself in a materialistic form. The manufacturing of the drug is modern-day sorcery.

I also remember yet another devastating episode of detoxing from drugs and alcohol when my wife of the present moment stood behind the semi-closed door of our bathroom in complete exhaustion from weeping and praying for God to intervene on my behalf. I was vehemently vomiting acidic fluids from my body that literally curled the toilet water as if it was boiling. The odor was so vile that it would create a dry heave that would within itself leave me gasping for my next breath, crying out to God to heal me or kill me. I didn't realize that He desired both as it was when I received a true revelation of God's redemptive work in Christ Jesus on Calvary's Hill that I received my healing.

I finally realized that Christ did not simply die for me, He died as me. I had lived most of my life under the thought that I was a sinner saved by grace. If this is true of you, let me say that you are not a sinner saved by grace. To be a sinner saved by grace, then your old man (old nature) is not dead. It is only when you can wrap your mind in the truth of redemption can you identify in Christ's death. It is as different as knowing of Jesus or knowing Him on a personal intimate level. You can know who He is, but not know Him as savior. John the Revelator did just that as he was on the island of Patmos in the Book of Revelation. Notice that Revelation is in singular form, and the one single focus is Jesus Christ. Patmos is defined as "the place of my death." John was exiled to this place to be put to death for the cause of Christ.

Revelation is the only book in the Bible that plainly tells you what it is about in the very first verse of chapter one—"the revelation of Jesus Christ"

Revelation 1:2

"Who testifies to everything he saw—that is, the word of God and the testimony of Jesus Christ." (NIV)

Note that it says, "The word of God and the testimony of Jesus Christ." This testimony is the revelation itself of the power of redemption. When we see Revelation for what it is, we then become like John and fall to the feet of Jesus as dead (Rev. 1:17).

So, my killing was my healing, and it was when I became identified with Christ in His death. You cannot be resurrected into newness of life until you become identified with Christ in death. I am getting way ahead of myself and drifting from the story of Job, or am I? Although this chapter speaks of a process of grieving, the Book of Job also ends with a beautiful picture of the work of

---

You cannot be resurrected into newness of life until you become identified with Christ in death.

---

restoration and redemption. Quickly, let me say that it is all about identification. Identity reveals authority—knowing who you are.

Relating back to the previous experience, as I was lying in silence on my bathroom floor that night, my wife, Kimberly, became traumatized to the point that she feared for my life. My body lay in the pool of sweat and overflowed toilet water as I jerked from intense seizures. The moments of unconsciousness would be interrupted from moments where I would begin growling like a mother bear protecting her cubs. There was a spiritual warfare that was going on inside of my soul. I was dying spiritually. I would like to say it was where I became totally identified in the work of redemption.

To only know the work of redemption from the viewpoint of what Christ did for you does not change you into a new creation. It only leaves you in an old mindset that continues to keep you in bondage to an old way of living. It's like those of the Old Covenant whose lives were wasted in a wasted howling wilderness wandering around in circles just simply trying to survive until a "someday" crossing over a river into a so-called promised land of rest. Believe me when I say there is no rest for the weary. I speak from experience, as I have spent the last 37 years of my life wondering if my life would ever end! A short poem that I wrote approximately 18 year ago gives witness to my wilderness journey.

"The Book"

My life, a book.
Another day, turn the page.
Today a new chapter begins.
Does this book never end?

As I once again survived the attack of my physical and mental episode of detoxing, one would think that this event alone would cause a person to come to his end. Let me say that your end was at Calvary, but until you step into the reality of redemption, you will continue to live in bondage.

The saga continued. It is in these moments when you don't see the internal healing taking place. It is where we become blind to the personal work of Jesus in our lives because of the physical and mental pain that leaves one twisted like a hard-baked pretzel under the weight of failure. The only quick fix is to use again. The problem with this self-help method of self-medicating is that you never know when or where you will crash again. I once crashed while sitting in a barber chair. When I regained a temporary consciousness, I jumped up and ran out of the barber shop. I just made it to my truck and drove off as the EMS team was pulling in. These events would create extreme embarrassment to the point I would re-locate geographically.

Let we say that your end was at Calvary, but until you step into the reality of redemption, you will continue to live in bondage.

The most devastating event that I had experienced was when I was found in the floor of the Georgia Tech basketball facility in Atlanta, Georgia. I was taken outside where two different EMS teams awaited me, refusing medical attention that was available on the scene. I called my sister who lived close to the campus to come drive me to our parents' house that was 45 minutes north of Atlanta. As we were exiting the interstate, she attempted to take me to yet another hospital in Cartersville, Georgia. Once again, I refused. I did not have a desire to live. However, after morning came, I was walking across the backyard to feed my hounds when I collapsed to the ground. I then agreed to receive medical attention. The aorta had collapsed, and I was not receiving oxygen to my heart. This was also during a time I had broken my T-11 vertebrae in my back.

While still in our home in Arkansas, my wife and I were bream fishing when a large cottonwood tree uprooted from the banks of the water's edge. The tree fell on me driving me and our boat completely underwater. I was momentarily trapped beneath the water's surface. I was later rescued and rushed to Memphis, Tennessee for medical attention. I share these events that have taken place in my life, not to glorify myself, but to give glory to a merciful God who has lavished me with grace—to show how God's redemptive work in His Son sits in wait for us to realize what is already true of us. His grace is what provided a way out for me. Unmanaged grief produced a destructive and lonely lifestyle for this simple country boy.

Have you, like myself, become exhaustive in your vain attempts of self-effort to change? Have you, like myself, found yourself unable to properly function in other areas of your life? Then please adhere to my advice when I suggest to you that we do not have to expect more of ourselves than what we can handle in our times of grief. Grieving is what Job did. Good grieving is designed to bring healing and comfort. It also brings closure. Unmanaged grief results in violence, anger, sickness, and physical diseases. This is proven by medical science. My physical diseases were heart failure, diabetes, high blood pressure, and arthritis.

> *Have you, like myself, become exhaustive in your vain attempts of self-effort to change?*

Silence is not easily accomplished. We have spent the majority of our lives sweeping things under the rug with a mentality that says, "Out of sight is out of mind." This is far from the truth. Unmanaged grief is deceptive in nature. In order for change to take place we must move from a place of self-deceit into an honest disclosure. Although Job pleaded to God for answers as to "why," he also maintained an awareness of God's power to save him. He did not hide his emotion; he expressed them!

―――――――――――――――――――――――――――――――――――

God does not make bad things happen so He can teach us a lesson. Lessons are learned through the events that happen to us.

―――――――――――――――――――――――――――――――――――

Job's friends clung to a mere common view that is still practiced today. That view is what I call "sin searching." Just because someone is going through traumatic times does not necessarily mean they have done something wrong. The watchwords are self-responsibility and personal accountability. More times than not, we search for something or someone to blame. In my own case, I blamed myself. There may be moments in which we just might need a little self-blaming, but when dealing with others, we need to remember that they too may need their moments to indulge in "the blame game." In other words, the blame game works both ways!

This is best seen in Job 7:11-21. Throughout Job's trials and tribulations, God was ever present. God did not make these events happen to Job, no more than He causes bad things to happen to good people. What He will do is show up and show out in the lives of those who call upon His name. God does not make bad things happen so He can teach us a lesson. Lessons are learned through the events that happen to us. Events happen under their own steam and as random as raindrops on a rainy day. However, it is our storms where God is ever present—not the cause of the storms. It is in His presence where I found my change. As I have also previously stated, "Real change is an exchange—your life for His."

The choice is yours.

Chapter Three

THE MERRY-GO-ROUND
(A Cry for Change)

When I began reading in the Book of Ecclesiastes, I quickly began to recognize how the thoughts of King Solomon ran an incredible parallel with my own as I tried to analyze life in my self-efforts to find meaning. Solomon's self-effort attempts for happiness were much the same as many of us today. We seek to fill the God-shaped void in our lives with work achievements, alcohol and drug use, wealth, and the most common of all, relationships. Matthew 16:26 tells us, "What good will it be for someone to gain the whole world, yet forfeit his soul...?" (NIV)

Solomon, like myself, not only hit a bottom, but he wallowed in his bottom (God likes it when we hit rock bottom because it is there that we realize He is the rock of the bottom!). However, it is in these bottoms where revelation occurs. It's where we come to realize that without God in our lives and an understanding of His redemptive work in Christ Jesus, our lives will resound the words of Solomon that are found in chapter one verse two: "meaningless, meaningless—utterly meaningless."

Solomon's cry for change found throughout the Book of Ecclesiastes echoes the words, "Vanity, vanity—all is vanity." He had been caught up into the mundane of everyday living. He, like most of us today, was in search of something more than he was experiencing. He was caught up in the mentality that nothing was new under the sun. No one is exempt from the thought of "there has to be more than I have experienced." For the majority of my life, I have often said these words, both silently in thought and with an outburst of frustration openly before others and directed to God, "There had to be more!"

Remembering my childhood years in a small southeastern Missouri town of Hayti, Missouri where I lived on the north end of town just outside the city limits and just a couple of blocks from the city park, there was an old merry-go-round. It seemed the most popular thing in the park for kids. Not only would it be full of kids, but kids would surround the merry-go-round to wait for the next ride. When the merry-go-round would slow to an almost stop, the drunken kids would fall off their seats and stagger away. The rush of the crowd to board the next ride would always leave one in sadness. I seemed to always be the one to give up my seat to the broken-hearted. In doing so, I had to be the one to push the ride into motion. I would grab hold of the smooth metal rail and begin pushing. As the merry-go-round was pushed into motion, the shouts of "Faster! Faster!" would fill the air. I began pushing faster and faster to the point of total exhaustion that would leave me collapsing to the ground unable to catch another breathe. I would just lie there as my body poured sweat like an open faucet.

As I write this, I think of the times of detoxing from the drugs and alcohol that I mentioned in my previous chapter. I compare this, as well as the next thirty years of my life, to that of King Solomon's life that is revealed in the Book of Ecclesiastes, as I had previously stated. Solomon sought to achieve happiness and purpose in a way many of us still do to this day. We do so through drug/alcohol use, relationships, work, and money. Solomon hit bottom, and like myself, had come to a conclusion that it all was "meaningless, meaningless—utterly meaningless!" (Ecclesiastes 1:2).

Verse three of chapter two goes on to say, "What do people gain from all their labors at which they toil under the sun?" The question remains today of what does a man gain from his self-efforts (labors), as he pushes on the merry-go-round of life, as described in the remaining verses of chapter one. Questions with no answers are what seem to be ever so common in our fast-paced lives—questions that seem to absorb the today but forgotten in the tomorrow. There are, however, questions that need answers, and such questions about meaning and purpose hold value. These questions need not be lost. If they become lost, we will also lose track of who we are both in depth and direction. Our depth and direction are what produces vision. Scripture tells us that without a vision, we will perish. This is what happened to me. I lost my identity, and my vision became tainted by the resounding words of "meaningless, meaningless—utterly meaningless!" For years, I avoided answering the central question of my life—"who am I?"

Questions with no answers are what seem to be ever so common in our fast-paced lives—questions that seem to absorb the today but forgotten in the tomorrow.

Change can and will take place in one's life without permission—such changes as when my thoughts of a good life "under the sun" changed to a life of laboring "in the sun." My question of "who am I," changed to "why me." Once again I'm reminded of the words of my pastor, Darrell Gooden, when I asked the all too famous question, "Why me?" He had asked me to repeat the question three times in a row. I did as he said, repeating "why me, why me, why me?" As he laughed and walked away, he replied, "Sounds like you're just 'why-ning to me." I thought it as a joke, only to realize now what he was actually saying to me that day.

The "who, why, and what" syndrome had found residency in my life and became ever-present in my thoughts.

- Who am I? (Identity Crisis).

- Why me? (Emotional Crisis).

- What now? What am I doing? (Vision Impaired).

A person's identity is not based on what they do.
Although I have been identified as a 'drunk' and/or a
'meth head,' they have nothing to do with who I am.

I was perishing in the wind as I became enslaved to the mundane of everyday life in the sun, asking the repetitive question, "Is there anything new?"

My childhood life on a merry-go-round had permeated my life as an adult. My self-efforts seemed to be the right thing to do but always left me burned out. There were achievements that took place in these burned-out moments of my life. I now realize that the reason I did not realize them then is because of my absence in those moments. As usual, when I realized it, it was too late. My conclusion was always that my labor wasn't worth the wage.

My unrealistic goals and my grandiose way of thinking only left me frustrated to the point I would simply give up. My pursuit of happiness was fueled by excessive consumptions of drugs and alcohol and always ended in disappointment. I call it the "executive burn-out." The executive burnout is that of one who never really experiences success. I was one that seemed to always be just short of reaching success, and my anger would be what dominated any ambition I would have for success. This is also seen in the second chapter of Ecclesiastes.

The good life that I often portrayed was only pretending. Again, change took place without permission. My life's central question had changed from 'who am I' to 'why me' to 'what am I doing?' Was I acting or pretending? Either way, I was living under a false identity. A person's identity is not based on what they do. Although I have been identified as a 'drunk' and/or a 'meth head,' they have nothing to do with who I am. They are titles that people place on me, and others based on what we did. Your job or your activities are not who you are; they are what you do. With this misrepresentation of my identity, my life that I lived was only pretending, and the world that I lived in became my stage.

> "I might have done what they said I did, but I'm not who they say I am." ~Bishop David Huskins

I see this pretention in church settings as well. We all are guilty of pretending—all as in sinner and saint; believer and non-believer; religious and non-religious. We all have been guilty of covering up our dirt of the past as well as the present. These self-efforts of covering up only leaves us burned out on the religious merry-go-round screaming, "Insanity, insanity." We all suffer from insanity.

My pursuit of happiness was fueled by excessive consumptions of drugs and alcohol and always ended in disappointment.

Insanity is defined as continuing to do the same things over and over with an expectation of different results. Spiritual insanity is defined as getting saved by grace and then returning to trying to stay saved by the "do's and don'ts" of modified religious behavior. In true country boy terms: "If you keep doing what you've always done, you're only going to get what you always got." Spiritually speaking, you're going to continue to get beat up by the Bible. If anyone is using the Bible to beat you up, they are using it the wrong way. I would often find myself in my little make-believe world pretending to be someone else, doing something else, in a distant land of somewhere else. It's like going on a trip but never leaving the farm.

As my high life would check into reality, I would always have a feeling of failure. I would always feel as my present circumstances were a mistake, and I would fall for the lie that my life itself was utterly meaningless.

Spiritual insanity is defined as getting saved by grace and then returning to trying to stay saved by the "do's and don'ts" of modified religious behavior

---

As I continue to read into chapter three of Ecclesiastes, I see where Solomon had concluded that there is a time for everything. We all know the story:

- A time to be born, and a time to die.
- A time to plant, and a time to harvest.
- A time to kill, and a time to heal.
- A time to tear down, and a time to build up.
- A time to weep, and a time to laugh.
- A time to mourn, and a time to dance.
- A time to scatter, and a time to gather.
- A time to embrace, and a time to refrain.
- A time to search, and a time to give up.
- A time to keep, and a time to throw away.
- A time to tear, and a time to mend.
- A time to be silent, and a time to speak.
- A time to love, and a time to hate.
- A time for war, and a time for peace.

All of these times are descriptive of the process of change. 'A time' is a moment, and we need to learn how to value each moment of our lives. We will not ever experience change by avoiding our moments. We experience change only when we surrender to and accept our moment. Moments, just as days, have their good and bad. However, Romans 8:28 states that "all things work together for good." We have to learn to trust the process of our ever-changing life. This trust is our faith in a loving and caring God who is for us and not against us.

Everything that we attempt to do in life always seems promising at first. As this promising begins to diminish, and our self-efforts become intensified by our works-based mentality, we become more aware of its deception. Our working to achieve is often related to our exploring the world for pleasure instead of searching our souls for meaning. Nothing of this world will ever have meaning until we get a real revelation of Jesus Christ and the finished work of redemption.

Wisdom is what King Solomon had asked God for. His wisdom became foolish talk when he leaned on his own self-efforts to understand life. Real wisdom is best represented when we depend on God Himself for our change. Our change should be effortless as our lives become saturated with the aggressive forgiveness of grace.

The choice is still yours.

"I might have done what they said I did, but I'm not who they say I am." ~Bishop David Huskins

---

Chapter Four

THE CALL TO PREACH

"He who disregards his calling will never keep the straight path in the duties of his works" ~John Calvin

As I sit in a moment of silence, my thoughts travel back through time to an old white two-story house that stood on a corner lot just a few blocks from downtown Hayti, Missouri. Hayti is a small country town that is located in the extreme southeast corner of the state that is known as the Bootheel of Missouri. Just across the street was an old junkyard and a railroad track that ran north and south across town. As a child, I would explore the junk yard as if it were a jungle, and I was in search of a treasure. I would walk the railroad tracks for miles in search of new discoveries. I was a true "Tom Sawyer" without a river. I did discover later in life that the mighty Mississippi River lay just five miles east of the old white house.

I remember those childhood years as if it were yesterday. They were the best years of my life. It was in those years that I had no worries. All I knew was what I wanted to be when I grew up. I wanted to be a preacher just like my Dad. I remember a day when I first began to explore the junkyard—for what, I wasn't sure. However, I did meet three cats and a dog. I had found my treasure, as I now had a congregation to preach to. I jumped on top of an old emerald green car, and I began to preach to my new-found congregation. As I pretended to be like my Dad, I would say, "Come—welcome to the House of the Lord." To my surprise the congregation had immediately expanded! My audience was now seven birds, four cats, and two dogs! All went well for several days until I tried to baptize the cat. It felt more like I had just been crucified! I bore a few stripes that day, and that cat sent me home licking my wounds. I don't suggest to anyone to try baptizing a cat.

I would rather wake up a sleeping bear than to do that again. That cat didn't take very well to having the devil cast out of him, either. That cat is like some Christians of today. Some are just best left alone. I also realized that the attendance of my new-found congregation was best when I fed them.

It's funny how we are so quick to be reminded of the bad times in our lives but fail to remember when life was good—when our dreams had not yet been stepped on and were still alive inside our hearts

---

It was also on that day that as I was preaching the sermon that my Dad had preached the night before, I grabbed the antenna off that old car and leaped to the ground saying, "And the Spirit of the Lord came through like a mighty rushing wind!" By the time I said that, a horse came up behind me and blew. I jumped about four feet straight up in the air in an attempt to get back on top of that old car. I think this was when I first ever spoke in tongues!

After the initial shock was over, I heard a deep gravely, soft-spoken voice say, "Who are you preaching to there boy?" It was on that day that I met Frank Johnson. Frank was the owner of the junkyard. He was a thick-skinned old man who walked with more of a slide than a step. He had tobacco stains that ran down both sides of his chin and had the smell of hay and horse on his on-strapped overalls. His old leather boots were never tied, and his boot strings would wave in the wind. I stood speechless, and silence filled the air as he waited for my answer. All I could say was, "I like horses." It was on that day that I rode my first horse. I cried the day Frank Johnson died.

Memories are good at times, and this one brings a smile as I once again sit down to write of more of my life's lessons. It's funny how we are so quick to be reminded of the bad times in our lives but fail to remember when life was good—when our dreams had not yet been stepped on and were still alive inside our hearts. I was recently asked the question as to how old I was when I first realized I was called to preach. I just smiled and said, "That's easy; I was five." It was on top of an old emerald green car in a junkyard that sat next to the railroad tracks. It is where I was "called to preach."

It was also in that old two-story white house where I laid on the floor in front of the console TV and watched Neil Armstrong land on the moon. I remember the feeling that overtook me as I lay there in my pajamas. I thought that if a man could go to the moon, then surely I could preach.

It was also in that old house where I remember my mother reading Bible bedtime stories to my sister and me. My favorite story was that of Jonah and the Whale. I guess it was the fact of a man who had lived inside of a fish. I would drift off to sleep with those stories fresh on my mind. Often I would dream of preaching, and my sermons would always be a word for word repeat of my mother's voice. I could always see her smiling at me as if she knew I was called to preach.

I have always known of my calling, yet heeded it not because of the circumstances of my life that soon took place. It was in this same year that I would be molested by a man in full army uniform. He was the son of a friend of my Aunt Florence Frazier who lived down a long dirt road about thirteen miles north of Hayti. This event alone caused me to feel as I had done something wrong—wrong before the God of whom my mother taught me. I felt unworthy and dirty. I had entered the neighbor's home for the fact that my aunt did not have indoor plumbing, and I had been playing in the cotton fields. I had to relieve myself, and as I entered the bathroom, there he was masturbating. I stood frozen as I had never seen anything of the such. As I turned to run out of the bathroom, he caught me by the back of my shirt and pulled me back into the bathroom and locked the door latch that was just out of my reach. When he was done with me, he gave me a dollar and said,

"Whatever you do, don't tell anyone or God will strike you dead, or your mom and dad will send you away."

All of a sudden the God that my mother taught me, a God who was full of mercy and grace, had just turned into one of anger and vengeance. I would suggest that it just may be incidents such as this in others' lives that causes them to become dysfunctional. For some, it may be homosexuality, drugs, alcohol, etc. This should give reason for us Christians not to be judgmental of others. No one knows what season of life a person is in. Just as there are seasons in a calendar year, we also have seasons in our lives. First Corinthians 4:5 states,

> "Therefore judge nothing before the appointed time; wait until the Lord comes. He will bring to light what is hidden in darkness and will expose the motives of the heart." (NIV)

I once read a story of a Persian King who had four sons. He desired to discourage his four sons from becoming judgmental and critical of others. He sent each of his four sons on a journey to see a mango tree. He sent them one at a time in different seasons of the year—one for each season. Upon their return, each gave their description of what they saw. One said it to be a burnt old stump. Another said it to be beautiful and green. The third son described it as blossoming and beautiful. The youngest of the four sons said that its fruit was much like the pear. Then, the King replied, "You are all right! Each of you has seen it in its different seasons." The moral of this story is to judge no one, for you never know what season they are in. I was in my winter season, and my life reflected it. I became as a dried up old stump.

All of a sudden the God that my mother taught me, a God who was full of mercy and grace, had just turned into one of anger and vengeance.

Other circumstances that would take place would become a fuel for the destruction of my dream to preach. I had become entangled in the judgment trap. I judged others as well as myself. In First Corinthians 4:3-4, the Apostle Paul gives us good sound advice. He cautions us to not even to judge ourselves. However, it does say that God does the judging, and I felt like I had been convicted of a crime that I did not commit.

Throughout my life, I would hear the voice of God speak to me to tell someone of who He is, or He would put it on my heart to speak to them an encouraging word. Often I would keep my mouth shut because of the condition I was in. I would tell God, "Not now; I'm too high," or "I'm too drunk to tell them anything about You!" I would refuse and turn to go in the opposite direction. There was an incident that happened to me one night, and after that night, I never refused again. I had been clean from drugs and alcohol for about two months.

"They ought to get what they deserve!" Needless to say, we have—and we have paid dearly for the wrongs that we have done.

I was living in the Cedartown, Georgia area at the time. A young lady and I decided to get high, and we began drinking. We wanted to get out of town and go do some dancing. We traveled for about two hours or better to get way out of bird's-eye view of anyone who was connected to our church or our recovery center friends. We went north to Jasper, Georgia where I knew several people who I once partied with. Upon our arrival at the Blue Rodeo Bar and Dance, I was immediately drawn to another young lady who was on the dance floor. God spoke to me and gave me a prophetic word for her. I said, "Really, God? You have to be kidding!"

I went to the bar and ordered a double crown on the rocks and began reuniting with my old crowd. As I sat at the bar, a gentleman came up to me and with him was the young woman who had caught my attention upon my arrival. The man introduced himself along with the young lady. He stated that they were not together, and she wanted to dance. I refused and asked them to leave me be. They followed me around like two lost pups for the next several hours. After I asked them for about the third time to please leave me alone, God spoke again the words of the prophecy that I was to tell her. Only this time, I was rude and told them to leave me alone.

I left the bar to go to a friend's house to party the night out until daylight. When I entered the door, I looked into the living room and there she was. I turned and walked out and demanded the lady that was with me to get in the truck. As we were leaving, I was a good twenty-five miles down the Interstate when someone was riding my bumper and flashing their lights. I pulled over and jumped from my truck with a pipe in my hand ready to fight. This was not uncommon for me in this regard. The man got out and got on his knees with a card in his hand saying, "Please listen to me; I'm just a preacher!" A preacher? What the hell does a preacher want with me, and why was he in a bar? He went on to explain how he had backslid, and the young woman was someone he picked up that night as she was walking down the road. He stated that God spoke to him that He had given me a word for her, and if I would please do so, then he and I would get some relief.

I spoke the words to her, and as I was speaking, the man began asking for forgiveness. The young woman opened her door and fell on her knees, and on the side of the highway, she received Jesus Christ as her personal savior. I know not where they are today, but about ten years ago, a friend of mine said that she was married, had kids, and attends church regularly. The man had returned to the pulpit, and his message of do's and don'ts had now changed to one of mercy and grace. It's funny how we can go somewhere, get out of town, and think we are hiding from God. Then He sends a backslidden preacher to where you are, and he gets a little booze in him and then starts talking about God!

My life had become a real life story much in the same as the bedtime story of Jonah that my mother read to me as a child. Jonah, as myself, had experienced a time where the word of the Lord had come. "The Word of the Lord came to Jonah..." (Jonah 1:1) Verse two states how God had told him to "go tell" just in the same way that night that He told me to "tell her." Jonah and I both turned in the opposite direction. Jonah boarded a ship, but I was getting ship-faced. The bottom line is that we both were disobeying a direct spoken word from God, and we were avoiding our call of duty. Jonah fled to Tarshish; I fled down the street as the storms stirred, and the ship we were in became beaten by the crashing waves of the seas. There were those around us that became frightened for their very lives. In Jonah's case, the ship's crew feared for their lives to the point that they cast lots to find out who was responsible for the calamity. As they cast lots, the lot fell on Jonah (Jonah 1:7). In my case, there were times when it would seem as all hell would break loose, and I knew it was the hand of God that was creating the crashing waves of my then lifestyle of drugs and alcohol.

My Nineveh was a people, a crowd that I had run with for thirty plus years—people who had heard of God, and some as myself knew that He could save us if only we would let go. My argument with God was, "Where do I send them if I did get them saved?" I only knew of a couple of churches that I would even recommend them to go to. And they seemed as if they were in a distant land of somewhere else.

Throughout the first four chapters of Jonah, we read of Jonah's resistance to go preach. He, like myself, made excuses and always expressed a need to be right and wanted everyone to praise him. How many of us today are still seeking that pat on the back, you're-doing-great praise from others? Affirmation can be good and is needed at times. But self-seeking praise is nothing more than an act of religion and is self-righteous in nature.

After God spared the life of Jonah, he expressed his gratitude; and, I can possibly testify that he was ready to preach repentance to the city. I say this only because I myself would be driven to go save the city after every life-threatening event that I would survive. All I wanted to do was go show people what God had done for me. This is not wrong, but there is a time for everything. Jonah, as myself, also reacted out of fear—fear that if we were to go preach a message of repentance and the people did not accept it, then I would have to run for my life. The fact that God could and would do what He said wasn't the issue. The issue was if God didn't do it immediately, I would not get out alive.

In Jonah's case, he went to Nineveh and preached repentance, and God showed them mercy and grace. However, Jonah was not satisfied with God's response and threw a temper tantrum that ended with a crossing of his arms and a puckered-out bottom lip as he sat down in anger at a place east of the city. He built himself a shelter and wanted to see what God was going to do to the city. When he saw that He showed Himself merciful, he became even angrier with God. Jonah had looked upon the people as vile and cruel and deserving of God's punishment—punishment even unto death. Jonah's response to God's mercy and grace is the same as most religious-minded people of today. They look upon people such as myself that have been enslaved to a selfish, self-centered lifestyle of drugs and alcohol with an attitude like Jonah's that says, "They ought to get what they deserve!" Needless to say, we have—and we have paid dearly for the wrongs that we have done.

Anger will cause you to become blind to God's goodness in your own life. How many are as guilty as Jonah? How many have left the confines of a church where God had placed them so that He could extend His hand of grace unto them in their life? How many have left a church in anger so that they can look back as Jonah did unto the city of Nineveh and were going to watch them "get what they deserved—as if they were at a last day's BBQ waiting to say, "I told you so!" It is much like the mentality of the disciples of Jesus when they asked Him if they were to call down the fire of heaven upon the people as did Elijah. Jesus said, "You know not the spirit you are of."

Jonah was blinded by His religious mindset to the point that he could not see the grace and mercy of God in his own life. Even in his anger and jealousy of what God had provided for the people of Nineveh, God also provided for Jonah a place of rest. God even caused a tree to grow to provide shade for him as he pouted. I would suggest that this tree is symbolic of Calvary's cross, as the cross is where we find rest. The cross is what has protected us from the heat of laboring in the sun.

God has also provided for us a tree. However, this tree is thousands of years old, massive in strength, and provides a place where we can find rest in the shadows of its mighty work of redemption change. It's a change all right; it changes everything! It will even change our attitudes towards others from a "you get what you deserve" to a "forgive them as you have forgiven me." We no longer seek mercy and grace only for ourselves when we do wrong, and justice for others when they do wrong.

God has also provided for us a tree. However, this tree is thousands of years old, massive in strength, and provides a place where we can find rest in the shadows of its mighty work of redemption change.

Our change creates a cry of forgiveness for all when our knowledge of God's mercy and grace changes its residency from between our ears to our hearts.

Romans 6:1b (MSG):

"...if we have left the country where sin is sovereign, how can we live in our old house there?
Romans 6:2b

We entered into the new country of grace--a new life in a new land."

"We have now moved into Graceland, and Adam (the nature of the flesh) has left the building." ~Dr. Lynn Hiles

This building is the City of God—the New Jerusalem (you and I).

"And I John saw the holy city, new Jerusalem, coming down from God out of heaven, prepared as a bride adorned for her husband" (Rev. 21:2, KJV).

We are the bride of Christ. The fact is, this marriage is not a someday, futuristic event; it is a present-day reality that you are already married to Him. This reality comes when you understand the work of redemption that took place on Calvary's Hill. Your "old man" Adam died, therefore, freeing you to legally marry another, Christ Jesus. You were united with Him in a holy matrimony unto death and unto resurrection. If you are not already married to Him now, then you do not have the right to use His name.

Our change should be effortless as our lives become saturated with the aggressive forgiveness of grace.

Chapter Five

WHAT'S YOUR NAME?

In closing chapter four, I stated, "If you're not already married to Jesus, then you do not have the right to use His name." A name denotes a nature, and there are only two natures—the nature of Adam (flesh) and the nature of Christ (Spirit). One is corruptible; the other is incorruptible. One is of heaven; the other is of the earth.

Knowing who we are is vitally important. Identity gives authority and is reason to know who you are. To put labels on people based on things they have done can create an embarrassment to the point that those whom you label become destructive both toward you and themselves. We as Christians need not label people based on what they do. As I mentioned in an earlier chapter, what we do is not who we are. We are all first and foremost children of God.

We're Overcomers

> "He who has an ear, let him hear what the Spirit says to the churches. To him who overcomes I will give some of the hidden manna to eat. And I will give him a white stone, and on the stone a new name written which no one knows except him who receives *it.* (Revelation 2:17, NKJV).

Notice here where it says "to him that overcomes..." We are all overcomers by the blood of Jesus Christ. When we get an understanding of the work of redemption, we will have received hidden manna. This manna is the same manna that fed the children of Israel as they wandered around the waste-howling wilderness. This manna was the body of Jesus Christ Himself. I would suggest that the hidden manna is related to the manna that was placed inside the mercy seat as a reminder of God's provision to the people even in their rebellious lifestyle. We are no different. At least I wasn't. I can look back and see where God was ever present in my life, even in the years that I was in total rebellion.

The white stone symbolizes to me of a changed law—a law that once began on a rock of brimstone that could only produce death but has now been purified by love. And our name—our new name that we have received—is a gift. Our new name is Christ. Yes, that's right; our new name is Christ. We are no longer in Adam as Adam died and was not resurrected in victory. Only Christ was resurrected, and He was resurrected into newness of life. He rose up inside of us (His Body). The white stone is a pure Law of Love. The stone that once covered the opening of the tomb had been rolled away. Its purpose was not so Jesus could walk out but so that we can walk in. The only way that we will ever become aware of our new nature is to walk into an empty tomb and see where our old nature was laid to rest.

The empty tomb was the real mercy seat. It was inside of the tomb where the manna was hidden. However, when the stone was rolled away, the manna was no longer hidden. When we remove the stone of the Law, we see before our very eyes the true work of redemption as complete and finished. When God instructed Moses to build the Tabernacle, He instructed him to first build the mercy seat. I say it is because it really is an inside-out change in our lives. It's about God coming to us instead of us coming to Him. I'm not saying we are not to come to Jesus, but I speak from personal experience when I say that when I thought I had found God, He actually found me. Let me get back to my intended topic for this chapter.

As I mentioned, there are two names that represent two natures. In these natures, we see where they represent two worlds, or allow me to say, two ages. The word "world" is by definition an "age." When Jesus was speaking to us through the Apostle Paul and said, "Be ye not conformed to this world, but be ye transformed," He was speaking of the age of the Law. Christ was standing in the end of the age or old world that was governed by the Law of Moses. What Christ was trying to get them to see was that He was soon to be crucified, and through the work of redemption, they would be transformed—changed. From the age of a religious system that based their salvation on "doing" into a new age of grace that changes the *doing* to *done*.

Just as there were two worlds, two names, two natures, there were (and seems to still be), two religions. The first follows a set of rules to modify their behavioral system. It is about them working to obtain salvation. The other is governed by grace. It is by this grace that we come to a realization that the work has already been done by Christ and His redemptive work is totally complete.

Now we have come to a point of change, and the decision is yours. You can continue on in futility and in vain attempts to accomplish the impossible, or you can do as I have done and just simply let go and let God. The most powerful statement I ever heard was when a complete stranger told me to just "let it happen." It is easy to say, "Let go," but it's easier said than done. Trust me, I know! I also have come to realize that it is easier to let go of something if you have something else to grab hold of. It's easier to let go on one hand, if you have another hand to hold. So, allow me to attempt to give you something to reach out and take hold of, so that you can let go of an old nature of sin.

You can continue on in futility and in vain attempts to accomplish the impossible, or you can do as I have and just simply let go and let God.

First Corinthians 15:45-49:

"So it is written, 'the first man Adam became a living being'; the last Adam is a life-giving spirit. The spiritual did not come first, but the natural, and after that the spiritual. The first man was of the dust of the earth; the second man is of heaven. As was the earthly man, so are those who are of the earth; and as is the heavenly man, so also are those who are of heaven. And just as we have borne the image of the earthly man, so shall we bear the image of the heavenly man." (NIV)

The theologian, Hermann Ridderbos stated:

"Adam and Christ stand against each other as the two great figures at the entrance of two worlds, two creations, the old and the new...and in their actions and fates, lie the decisions for all who belong to them, because all men are comprehended in them."

Adam and Christ both represent spiritual destinies and are best seen in Romans chapter five (suggested reading, Romans 5:11-21). Everyone has an identity, but I also know that there has been, and still is an identity crisis among (but not limited to) most Christian circles. Many say they are New Covenant Christians but turn right around and say, "I'm just an old sinner saved by grace." Praise God you are saved by grace, but when you say that you're an old sinner, you are re-identifying yourself with the nature of Adam.

In the nature of Christ, the focus is on what Christ Himself did and accomplished in the powerful work of redemption that will give your life significance.

You are saved by grace, but grace saved you from your sin. In the nature of Adam, your identity was based on personal instinct. It was based on human reasoning and reaction. In the nature of Christ, our identity comes with revelation. It is an empowerment of life. The nature of Adam focuses on self and what self can do or accomplish. It creates a spirit of competition with others instead of creating a community with others. The nature of Adam seeks for self-rewards. The nature of Adam is the nature of self-righteousness itself, and the Scriptures plainly say that self-righteousness is as filthy rags (Isaiah 64:6). I could preach right now on this topic alone! But I won't (smile).

The self-righteous nature of Adam—that is based on what a man/woman does and accomplishes—is viewed as personal success. In the nature of Christ, the focus is on what Christ Himself did and accomplished in the powerful work of redemption that will give your life significance. I have concluded that Adam was a "sissy" in the Garden of Eden, when he disqualified himself as a man. In this nature, he has also passed on to humanity (especially men) a natural tendency to avoid responsibility. I have done this my entire life up to this point where I have come to realize that Adam has died.

Praise God, you are saved by grace, but when you say that you're an old sinner, you are re-identifying yourself to the nature of Adam.

"My old nature really is dead and my new life in the nature of Christ is my residency. I no longer seek to sin search my life, as to do so, I would have to dig up a dead old man. In my now new nature I realize that I no longer have a past to be forgiven of, a memory to forget, or even a testimony to tell. I have only a dead man to leave buried. His story is not mine to tell." ~unknown

Romans 5:18-21:

"Here it is in a nutshell: Just as one person did it wrong and got us in all this trouble with sin and death, another person did it right and got us out of it. But more than just getting us out of trouble, he got us into life! One man said no to God and put many people in the wrong; one man said yes to God and put many in the right. All that passing laws against sin did was produce more lawbreakers. But sin didn't, and doesn't, have a chance in competition with the aggressive forgiveness we call *grace.* When it's sin versus grace, grace wins hands down. All sin can do is threaten us with death, and that's the end of it. Grace, because God is putting everything together again through the Messiah, invites us into life—a life that goes on and on and on, world without end." (MSG)

We see here in this passage of scripture where the result of the nature of Adam was based on his disobedience to God.

Genesis 2:15-17:

"The Lord God took the man and put him in the Garden of Eden to work it and take care of it. And the Lord God commanded the man, "You are free to eat from any tree in the garden; but you must not eat from the tree of the knowledge of good and evil, for when you eat from it you will surely die." (NIV)

We can choose to sin, but we cannot choose the consequence of our sin.

We see here in the last part of verse sixteen that God gave Adam the freedom of choice. He said, "You are free to eat from any tree in the garden." This included the tree of knowledge of good and evil. However, God made the statement that he must not eat from the tree of the knowledge of good and evil. It was at this point that God warned Adam of the consequence that would follow if he made a bad decision. As I have stated in previous chapters, we can choose to sin, but we cannot choose the consequence of our sin. Unlike Adam, who knew his consequence, we still have a choice to make. We have the same freedom as Adam to choose which tree we eat from. The crisis of our identity is from an eating disorder. We are still trying to feed off the tree of knowledge of good and evil.

Many still think that we are to pick the good and throw away the evil (bad). The problem is that what appears to be good and what is visibly evil are both bad fruit. What appears to be good is worse than what is visibly evil. It's called deception! Any fruit from the same root system will only produce itself.

Matthew 7:15-19:

"Watch out for false prophets. They come to you in sheep's clothing, but inwardly they are ferocious wolves. By their fruit you will recognize them. Do people pick grapes from thornbushes, or figs from thistles?" (NIV)

Let me stop here momentarily to say that this passage of scripture runs a remarkable parallel with the Genesis account of Adam and Eve as they stood in front of the tree of knowledge of good and evil.

Scripture goes on to say:

"Likewise, every good tree bears good fruit, but a bad tree bears bad fruit. A good tree cannot bear bad fruit, and a bad tree cannot bear good fruit. Every tree that does not bear good fruit is cut down and thrown into the fire."

I would suggest that there are no longer two trees. There is but one tree that still stands, though it has been stained in blood and has the smell of death upon it; but it stands in resurrection power!

I had been in a state of wonder for some time concerning the fact that Adam did not partake of the tree of life, and why was he even standing in the reach of the tree of knowledge of good and evil? I had just recently asked God to reveal something to me so that I could have a clearer understanding of this event that brought condemnation upon all of humanity. This is what He showed me in a dream. In this dream I stood in a slightly elevated position just behind Adam and Eve as they stood underneath the canopy of a massive beautifully leafed tree. From this tree hung what appeared to be ripened fruit (no, it wasn't apples). It was a fruit like none other I had ever seen. As Eve reached out to pick one, I started yelling, "No, no, do not eat it!" It was as if I was not there, and they could not hear my voice. I continued to beg them to not participate in eating the fruit of the tree. In desperation, to get their

I would suggest that there are no longer two trees. There is but one tree that still stands, though it has been stained in blood and has the smell of death upon it; but it stands in resurrection power!

attention, I shouted out, "No, please don't do it!" I shouted again saying, "There is another tree that will give you eternal life." As I began searching for the tree of life, I turned to see them both eating the fruit of the tree. I began running toward them in an attempt to stop them when I stumbled and fell. In this fall, I began smelling a terrible odor as if something was dead. It smelled like a mixture of a dead dog and burning flesh. If you have never been around death, there is an odor unlike any odor you have smelled, and burning human flesh is the worst I have ever smelled—and I have the scars to prove my claim.

As I began to look around for what was dead, I saw a dead old tree laying across the ground. It was what I stumbled over when I fell to the ground. I looked and saw pools of blood and bloodstains all over this tree. I also saw what looked like railroad spikes laying all around me, and I began to weep. I had just found the cross of Calvary's Hill. I then realized that there is no deception in ugly, and the Cross of Calvary was as ugly as it gets. However, it is what produced eternal life for all of humanity. The deception was what was beautiful and seemed to give life. Funny thing is that I had already passed that way before in search of the Tree of Life and did not stumble over it. It wasn't until I turned behind me and saw Adam and Eve eating the fruit of the tree did I run toward them and stumbled. I personally feel as it was in the very moment that Adam disobeyed God and made the decision to eat that Christ died on the cross. I know that Scripture tells us He was the Lamb slain from the foundation of the world, but I would also suggest the Garden of Eden was the foundation of humanity, and it was there where the true Lamb of God was slain.

The reason God had to put Adam out of the garden was for the simple fact that he could not overcome his guilt and shame, and nowhere do I read in scripture, from Genesis to Revelation, where Adam or Eve ever asked God to forgive them. Perhaps if they had, then God would have allowed them to remain in the garden and to eat from the Tree of Life and live forever in the presence of the Almighty.

Something that I just now realized as I am writing of my dream is where I stated that I had turned around to see. What I was really looking for was the cross, and I only found it when I turned to see. I know that I turned to see if Adam or Eve had partaken of the fruit of the Tree of Knowledge of Good and Evil.

As I continued to read the Genesis account of the Fall, God also showed me how I, like Adam, had become enslaved to condemnation of self by allowing shame to rule my life. Shame is what created my false identity. Shame is an emotion, and when not attended to properly, it will create a need for justification. This is found in people who believe that shame gives them permission to feel sorry for themselves. This is not true. Shame will keep you in the mess you are in. If there is good found in shame, it would only be found when you allow your shame to create in you humility. Shame can and will take over your identity and become demoralizing. This kind of shame is toxic and creates a need for "covering up." This is what took place with Adam and Eve in Genesis chapter three verse seven.

If there is good found in shame, it would only be found when you allow your shame to create in you humility.

Shame was the consequence of Adam's disobedience; and it was, and still is today, in many people's lives the power of sin. In chapter two, verse twenty-five of Genesis, it states, "The man and his wife were both naked, and they felt no shame." This was evident before the Fall. It says they were naked and not ashamed. Nakedness does not tell me they were not clothed, but it tells me that they were transparent. They were in a transparent relationship with each other, and with God. I personally suggest that they were clothed in the glory of God. In this glory, they saw only God Himself. Nakedness was what symbolized their true identity. It was when they knew who they were and had nothing to hide.

Let's now look at Romans 5:27:

"For if by one man's offense death reigned through the one, much more those who receive abundance of grace and of the gift of righteousness will reign in life through the One, Jesus Christ." (NKJV)

As I read this scripture, I can say that I myself have been affected by Adam's disobedience and have fallen into the same self-righteous spirit of spending a lifetime of covering up. I believe it is safe to say that we all have done so at one point or another in our lives. I still can't figure out why we all still have the tendency to allow this first half of Romans 5:17 control our lives. If we would not be so focused on the fall of man and focus on the resurrection of man, we could begin to live life in a forward motion.

I never could understand how ten people can come up to you and praise you for something or tell you that you looked nice, then one person mentions how ugly your shoes are, and you will let the opinion of the one override the opinion of the ten. This causes one to think less of their self than they should. 1 John 4:17 tells us that we are as He is.

If we were to continue to read in Romans 5:18

"Therefore, as through one man's offense *judgment came* to all men, resulting in condemnation, even so through one Man's righteous act *the free gift came* to all men, resulting in justification of life." (NKJV)

This scripture plainly tells us that we as new covenant believers are no longer under the judgment of condemnation. We have been freely given justification of life! Also, notice that it says, "Judgment came." This is not futuristic; it is past tense. Our judgment was on Calvary's Hill, and Jesus Christ took the penalty of our sin upon Himself and crucified it on the cross. When the crucifixion was done, He said, "It is finished." Then I believe God said, "I'm satisfied." The judgment was passed, the penalty was paid, and then all were buried. The result was justification was done, and we all stand in resurrection power. The only thing that did not stand in resurrection power was the nature of Adam.

Let me close by quoting Second Corinthians 5:17

"Therefore, if anyone is in Christ, the new creation has come: The old has gone, the new is here!" (Suggested reading: Second Corinthians 5:11-21). (NIV)

It's a decision for change. However, the decision is yours.

If we would not be so focused on the fall of man and focus on the resurrection of man, we could begin to live life in a forward motion.

Intermission

A FOREWORD TO THE NEXT FIVE CHAPTERS

In the next five chapters, I will be discussing the topic of "sonship." I will be using the story of the prodigal son that is found in the Book of Luke, chapter 15. This story was a parable that Jesus spoke to the Scribes and Pharisees in an attempt to reveal the true heart desire of God, and that was to bring "many sons unto glory."

Hebrews 2:9-10:

"But we do see Jesus, who was made lower than the angels for a little while, now crowned with glory and honor because he suffered death, so that by the grace of God he might taste death for everyone. In bringing many sons and daughters to glory, it was fitting that God, for whom and through whom everything exists, should make the pioneer of their salvation perfect through what he suffered." (NIV)

In the beginning of verse 9 where it says, "But we see Jesus, who was made a little lower than the angels," we need to know that the word "angels," though it is written in plural form, is actually singular in nature. It is translated as "Elohim." Elohim is the name of God Himself. When we read this in its true sense, we realize that Jesus was made just a little lower than God Himself. To know these simple truths changes everything! It also gives evidence of the importance of knowledge. Scripture says that His people perish from lack of knowledge. Satan does not want these truths to be revealed to you, because to know who you are and to know your rightful position as a son poses a threat to his reign in your life. There is nothing Satan would want more than to keep you in the bondage of a mentality of a slave. Let me say it this way—we are not created to simply be a servant in the house of God. Servitude is not the purpose for our redemption. It is for the purpose of a relationship, and from this relationship, we obtain rulership.

Romans 8:15 reads:

"The Spirit you received does not make you slaves, so that you live in fear again; rather, the Spirit you received brought about your adoption to sonship. And by him we cry, *"Abba,* Father." (Daddy, Daddy!). (NIV)

I have just recently transitioned into the second phase of the discipleship program here at the Center of Hope. In this transition, I was to pick a favorite memory verse and expound on it. Romans 8:15 took the honors (smiling).

We as new covenant believers are no longer under the judgment of condemnation.

If we are to continue reading into verse 15, we have witness that the spirit of God Himself testifies with His spirit that is within us, and we are then called "children" of God. In this moment, God cut a new covenant. Just as He became human in the bodily form of Jesus and became satisfied in His own self, He also has done the same in you and me. This new covenant is failure proof because God cut this new covenant with Himself. It is the power of redemption! It is called being "born again."

Luke 15:24:

"'For this son of mine was dead and is alive again. He was lost and is found.' So they began to celebrate." (NIV)

In this new birth, we are united with Christ in resurrection power. In this resurrection, we become rightful heirs of the Kingdom of God and the right to participate in the inheritance as sons. This inheritance is best descripted in Ephesians 1:3-5:

"Praise be to the God and Father of our Lord Jesus Christ, who has blessed us in the heavenly realms with every spiritual blessing in Christ. For He chose us in him before the creation of the world to be holy and blameless in his sight. In love he predestined us for adoption to sonship through Jesus Christ, in accordance with His pleasure and will." (NIV)

This inheritance rightfully belongs to us the moment we receive the spirit of sonship. It is to this subject of sonship that I want to explore over the next three chapters. In this exploring of sonship, my prayer is that it will create in you a desire for change. Allow me now to share with you the nuggets of truth that have forever changed my life.

Chapter Six

A WAYWARD SON

In the previous chapter, I stated that a name denoted a nature, and that there were two natures. In this chapter, I want to give emphasis to the new nature in which we now live. It is in this new life of Christ that we have received the nature of righteousness.

Romans 5:17:

"For if, by the trespass of the one man, death reigned through that one man, how much more will those who receive God's abundant provision of grace and of the gift of righteousness reign in life through the one man Jesus Christ!" (NIV)

The key words here are *much more* and *abundant.* There is so much more to life in this new nature than we have been experiencing. Even as professed born again Christians, there are still those who do not live in the abundance of God's provision. God's provision that is spoken of here is in the work of redemption that was completed in the death, burial, and resurrection of Jesus Christ. In this abundant provision that has been freely given to us, we have now the right to receive the gift of righteousness. One of the most feared scriptures from the Book of Revelation gives a beautiful description of this abundant provision.

Revelation 14:20:   (Words and phrases in brackets are mine).

"They were [speaking of us] trampled in the winepress outside the city, [Calvary's Hill] and blood flowed out of the press [Jesus], rising as high as the horses' bridles for a distance of 1,600 stadia." (NIV)

Sixteen hundred stadia is three hundred kilometers (one hundred eighty miles). Three hundred represents divine completeness. What this scripture is saying to us is that there was enough blood shed on Calvary's Hill in the work of redemption to cover everyone's sin that believe. We cannot receive God's abundant provision unless we come to believe that what God did in Christ was enough to redeem us from the chokehold of death that was a result of living in our old sinful nature of Adam.

Why then do so many professed Christians still live in lack? It is because of their lack of knowledge. Until we get a complete understanding of the powerful work of redemption, we will never live in God's abundant provision of grace and the gift of righteousness. When we receive this provision of grace and the gift of righteousness, we will begin to reign in life. There are those, such as myself, that have experienced death and even a resurrection but seemingly failed at walking in freedom.

I can't help but think of the story of Lazarus found in the book of John, chapter eleven. Lazarus was resurrected when Jesus commanded him to "come forth." In verse forty-three of chapter eleven, Lazarus came shuffling out. Although he was resurrected, he was still connected to the grave because of the grave clothes that he was wearing. Lazarus, like myself, was brought back to life. Lazarus and I both were unable to loose ourselves from the grave clothes that still had us bound. In Lazarus' case, Jesus spoke to those who were standing around with their jaws hung open and their eyes bulged out to "loose him, and let him go." So the next time you ask yourself or even make the statement to others, saying, "I don't know why he/she just can't get it." Then, maybe, just maybe, it is because Jesus is waiting on you to lose them and set them free. Let me say it this way—"help them take off their grave clothes."

My grave clothes had me bound, and my soul was crying out for help; but, no one could hear me. My grave clothes were camouflaged with the life patterns of fear, anger, shame, condemnation, and were trimmed with legalism. Like Lazarus, all I could do was "shuffle." I am also reminded of a time that I was placed in a mental hospital under a suicide watch. It was where I saw first-hand what is known as the *thorazine shuffle*. It is the saddest thing I have ever seen; people just shuffle up and down the halls of the mental hospital like in the movie, *The Living Dead*. Their eyes are empty and hollow looking, their skin a pale white, and most have slobber dripping from the corners of their mouths. Others have white foam so thick in their mouths that they get choked when attempting to talk.

Thorazine is a medicine that is used as a mood stabilizer. It is supposed to be used to aid in calming a person who is homicidal and/or suicidal. However, I also know that it has become misused in most mental facilities and is used in a way that psychiatric nurses and care persons avoid their responsibilities to actually care for the patients. It has become nothing more than a babysitter.

I testify to this because of an incident that transpired during my stay at the mental facility. It was at suppertime when a person was bullying another person and was trying to take their food. As usual, I had to stand up for the less fortunate one. In doing so, I got into a verbal dispute, and before I knew it, I was inoculated! Trust me when I say that it's not a joke! It's a mood modifier alright. It's the next thing to never-never land. You become the living dead, and the only function is a shuffle—the thorazine shuffle.

It was in this moment of my life that I realized that I was in a pigpen, and I was feeding the swine. I had hit rock bottom, and as I began regaining my senses, I knew that I had to get back to my father's house. I speak of my natural father that lived about an hour or so just north of the Tanner Mental Health Facility in Villa Rica, Georgia. Spiritually speaking, I also knew that I had to get back to trusting God, and I began to lay out a plan to do so. The day that my father and Sims came to pick me up, I literally went for the front door. Sims spoke and said, "Wait a minute, before you leave here, I need to know what we are going to do next?" It was then that I knew I had to do something. I replied, "Where is that Christian-based rehab in Alabama?" His reply was, "It's not a rehab; it's a discipleship program, and it's in Anniston, Alabama, called Center of Hope." This was in 2014, just a couple of years ago. This event brings to my remembrance the powerful story of the Prodigal Son that is found in the Book of Luke. I will be referring to the prodigal as "the wayward son."

I was fifteen years old—the year was nineteen seventy-nine when tragedy hit our family. It was the year when I was involved in the tragic automobile accident that claimed the lives of my grandfather, William Henry Meadors; my grandmother, Evie Lorine Meadors; my aunt, Dixie Meadors Horst; and my infant cousin, Pamela Horst. Another cousin, Richie Horst, and I were the only two survivors of our vehicle. It was on that Saturday morning on June the ninth in the year nineteen seventy-nine that my life would take a sudden 180 degree turn around, and my wayward ways began. Out of this incident, I had received around $6,000 from my grandfather's insurance. In the story of the wayward son, the son had asked his father for his share of the estate. I will also be using the word *inheritance* in place of estate. Keep this word in your thoughts as you continue to read.

Luke 15:12 (Words in brackets are mine):

"The younger son [the wayward son] said to his father, 'Father, give me my share of the estate [inheritance]. So he [the father] divided his property between them." (NIV)

Here we see where the father divided his property or estate (inheritance) between two sons. In verse thirteen, it tells how the wayward son, like myself, gathered up all he had and left home. In the beginning of my senior year in high school, I decided that I wanted to be my own man and moved in with some of my friends.

I had no contact with my parents for almost nine months. This was really the beginning of my wayward ways.

When I was eighteen years old, I graduated from high school with $6,000 and a Chevy Luv pick-up truck. I was ready to live it up! I bought new clothes, had a checking account, and was ready to woo the ladies. However, it wasn't long until the checks were bouncing. The bank closed my account, and my truck was broken down. I was living wherever I could lay my head.

Verse fourteen of chapter fifteen says it best:

"After he had spent everything, there was a severe famine in the whole country, and he began to be in need." (NIV)

This event was the first of a life-long series of events that would always leave me in need. I had a restless spirit—a wayward lifestyle. Each time I would always find myself in a pen just as this wayward son did in verse fifteen.

"So he went and hired himself out to a citizen of that country, who sent him to his fields to feed pigs." (NIV)

Many times I sold myself short and would take any job that I could just to make a few dollars. The worst job I ever did was cleaning out soured soybeans out of a granary dump station. I had to go down into a pit where the soured soybeans stood knee deep and smelled worse than a dead dog. I had to dip them out with a five-gallon bucket that was tied to a rope so that my co-worker could raise it out of the pit and empty the beans in a wheelbarrow. The wheelbarrow was then rolled around to the back of the granary and dumped in a pile. Eventually, they would be placed into 55-gallon drums that would sit on the back of a pick-up truck. The truck would then be driven to hog lots and dumped in feed troughs. The soured grain would be full of maggots (the size of grub worms) and the drippings from the bucket. As it was pulled out of the pit, it would find its way into my boots, pockets, and shirt.

It didn't take me long to "come to my senses," as the wayward son did in verse seventeen.

Let me back up briefly to verse sixteen:

"He longed to fill his stomach with the pods that the pigs were eating, but no one gave him anything" (Luke 15:16, NIV)

The wayward son took his inheritance, spent it, found himself in need, got a job feeding pigs, and now he has become hungry. It was here where he came to his senses. Let me say that hunger has a way of making a person rethink their situation. Hunger has a way of changing your mind. In his desperation, he began to examine his situation. He began to remember how good it was in his father's house. He began smelling the smells of home. For me, it was beans cooking on Mom's stove; the smell of cornbread in the oven; and, the smell of potatoes and onions frying on the stove top in a ten-inch iron skillet. It was while I was still miles from home, broke and no way to go—not even a quarter for a phone call (no cell phones then)—that I decided to return to my father's house. I would walk for miles in hopes that someone would stop and pick me up. During this time of walking, I would rehearse speeches much like that of the wayward son in verse eighteen.

"I will set out and go back to my father and say to him: Father, I have sinned against heaven and against you."

I remember a time that I had a serious automobile accident due to being extremely drunk. It took me 12 hours to find my father's house, and I was only fifteen minutes away. When I arrived, I began praying and prophesying to myself. I have asked my dad to give his account of this event and this is what he stated:

"Kenny showed up at our house sometime around 3:00 AM. When I met him in the carport, he was crying and begged me to hug him. I was aggravated because of his drunken condition, and I reluctantly gave him a hug. You have to understand my frustration that caused me to later come to the realization that I was loving Kenny conditionally. I showed love to him if he was doing "right" and withdrew my love when he was doing "wrong." It took me years to finally come to the realization that Kenny was my son, and I was going to love him regardless. It was several years later that I communicated my love for Kenny even though I did not approve of his misdeeds. I now see this is no doubt how our Heavenly Father sees us.

I saw that Kenny was in a lot of emotional and physical pain. When I took him to the emergency room, it was discovered that he had a broken collar bone. He apparently registered a high alcohol level, because the hospital had called the State Highway Patrol. When the patrolman arrived at the hospital, he immediately charged Kenny with (Driving under the Influence (DUI). They had no proof that he had been driving under the influence, but they assumed that he must have been since he was drunk and was injured.

What is interesting from this incident is that I was the pastor of a local church and was very jealous of my identity that I did not want to be marred. You see, my name is William Kenneth, and Kenny is Kenneth Larry. I always thought Kenny prided himself as being Kenneth Meadors, as that was what I was always known. The local newspaper always listed any arrests, and of course, I was concerned that Kenneth Meadors would be listed and be mistaken for me. That would have been devastating to my pride and namesake. I called a lady who was a prayer warrior telling her of my concern. Guess what—there was no report of the arrest in the newspaper! By the way, I think I could have been justified in my concern, as people immediately draw their conclusions and do not change their opinion of you when falsely charged even though it may be discovered later that you were not the culprit.

Kenny had been shown the grace and mercy of God so many times, and I think he credited most of that to his mother's prayers. This time was no exception, as he was completely exonerated of all charges of DUI! This was one of the first of many misgivings of Kenny due to alcoholism. I can testify that it has been a rough journey for my wife and me in dealing with the curse of alcoholism in our family. But, thanks be to God, I now believe with all my heart that Kenny has truly turned his life around for the glory of God."

My speeches were usually more directed to my Mom. My brother Lyle and I knew the quickest way back in the house was through our Mom. If we could sound pitiful enough to Mom, Dad couldn't stand a chance. I know now that my father longed to see us as much as Mom did. I know that he spent many hours pacing the floors in wait for a phone call. Our coming home may not have seemed as kosher as the return of the wayward son as written in verse twenty, but we both were always welcomed. Note in verse twenty-one where the wayward son began his well-prepared speech of acceptance. He had barely gotten his speech spoken when the volume of the father's voice began to drown out his words with words spoken to his servants,

"Quick! Bring the best robe and put it on him. Put a ring on his finger! Put sandals on his feet! Bring the fattened calf and kill it! It's time to celebrate with a feast of thanksgiving!" (paraphrase mine).

Verse twenty-four states:

"For this son of mine was dead and is alive again; he was lost and is found. So they began to celebrate." (NIV)

There is no better story than this to describe the power of redemption (in my opinion). Everything that the father spoke concerning the return of his son is depictive of New Covenant blessings. Let's look specifically at verses twenty-two through twenty-four:

> "But the Father said to his servants, "Quick! Bring the best robe and put it on him. Put a ring on his finger and sandals on his feet. Bring the fattened calf and kill it. Let's have a feast and celebrate. For this son of mine was dead and is alive again; he was lost and is found.' So they began to celebrate. (NIV)

I have known this story since my childhood and have read it on numerous occasions. I have heard it preached from the pulpits and even preached it myself. However, it has not been until about two years ago that God began revealing an in-depth understanding of the entirety of this story. I would have to also include the parables of *The Lost Sheep* and *The Lost Coin.* All three have a powerful message that reveal the "Father's Heart."

The father's expression to his son was one of acceptance. This acceptance was an "as-is" acceptance. My thoughts are that the wayward son was still covered in "doo doo—pig poo." I do not read anywhere that would suggest that the son was showered and shaved, but he definitely had the smell of doo-doo on him. It was in this condition that the father wrapped the best robe around him. This robe was not an ordinary garment. Robes were for special occasions and were also used for exchange when a covenant was cut between two parties (best seen in the story of David and Jonathan, 1 Samuel 18).

The placing of this robe around his son was a sign of restoring his position as a son. As the process of restoration continued, the next event that took place was the placing of a ring on his finger. This is symbolic of the restoration of authority. This

We will perceive ourselves wrongly if we have a wrong concept of God.

was the restoring of a forfeited right of the son by the authoritative right of a father. The sandals were symbolic of restored honor—honor of a son, as no servant wore sandals. These were all gifts that a father would give only to his son. They were all gifts of restoration. Now here's the meat!—the fatted calf!

As I stated, I had read this story and had heard it as preached from a traditional point of view that always said, "Go kill the fatted calf!" This is not what it says. It says, "Bring the fatted calf here and kill it." I suggest that the father restored his son at the very place that he embraced him, and then he ordered his servants to bring the calf to him and kill it. I personally feel that the father was saying to himself, "The buck stops here!"

I would suggest that the intent of the father's heart was to not allow his son to take another step until his covenant (New Covenant) was sealed by the shedding of blood. Will you agree with me now when I say that this story is a beautiful picture of the work of redemption that God completed in His Son on Calvary's Hill?

MEANWHILE...

Meanwhile speaks of something that was taking place at the same time as the celebration. While the celebration of the homecoming was in full swing, there was another son who was working (Luke 15:25). As his work brought him closer toward the house, he heard the sound of music and of dancing. Out of curiosity he asked a servant what was taking place. It's funny to me that this older son was so entangled with being about his father's business that he couldn't even take time to go see for himself what was going on. This reminds me of a quote from the movie, "The Book of Eli," where Denzel Washington made the statement, "I have been so busy defending the book (the Bible) that I have not been doing what it says to do!" The younger wayward son had come to his senses and realized that he was wrong. This older son also had a problem, but he failed to recognize it. They both had a wrong perception of their father.

We will perceive ourselves wrongly if we have a wrong concept of God. The ministry of Jesus was to unveil the true nature of God. The true heart of God longs to love you, and He awaits your return home. I was hungry, angry, lonely, and tired, and I began to talk to God. My words were not fancy, nor were they all clean. I was angry and used wild words in my conversation with God. Because of my loneliness, I wept with a brokenness of heart. I was tired, so I slept.

I would have to say that God performed His best work in me as I slept. I say this for the fact that as I was awake, I was too busy telling Him all that was wrong in my life. I can honestly say that the day I left my home in Arkansas to return to the Center of Hope, I knew I had just made the best decision of my life. That decision was to give God my all—all as in all—every situation, every thought, and every ideal. I turned my life over to Him to do with it as He saw fit. What else did I have to lose? Nothing at all, except a concept—a wrong concept of who I was. The only thing that I have lost is fear.

When I was giving it my all—and it seemed as if my all wasn't good enough—I could not see the reward of my efforts and never understood why I never could see the fruits of my labor. The truth is you cannot receive from God a reward that already belongs to you by inheritance. The robe, the ring, and the sandals of the wayward son were all gifts from the Father. However, they did not become gifts upon his return. They were gifts that were already purchased through the shed blood of Jesus as He hung suspended on Calvary's cross. I have concluded that these gifts had already been given to the Son and lay in wait for His return.

Ephesians 1:3:

"Praise be to the God and Father of our Lord Jesus Christ, who has blessed us in the heavenly realms with every spiritual blessing in Christ." (NIV)

Welcome home, my brothers and sisters—it's time to celebrate! The party has started, and the new wine of the New Covenant is flowing!

Chapter Seven

WHAT YOU SEE IS WHAT YOU GET

As I continue to read and reread the parable of the prodigal son, I realize that with each reading I experienced healing in my mind, body, and soul. There truly is a hidden treasure found in this passage of scripture. Nugget after nugget of truths of who I am continue to be found. I feel like I'm back in the old junkyard that I once roamed as a kid. I thumb through scripture in search of new things—new understanding that causes a change in my perspective of who I am. In my treasure hunt through the Book of Luke, I realized that Luke's purpose was to present to us the true love of Jesus and His compassion for all of humanity. However, Jesus' purpose was to reveal the heart of the Father so that we can understand who we really are and what rightfully belongs to us.

> *If we don't see ourselves worthy, we will never experience the acceptance of the Father.*

In chapter six, I touched on the prodigal (wayward) son and how he asked the father for what was his share of his inheritance. He gathered what he thought was his and headed out for a distant land to live it up under the sun. There is no evidence to the length of time that it took for him to squander his wealth and to hit bottom. In this bottom, he became hungry and in need. In this moment of need, he, like myself, was willing to sell himself short just to satisfy a hunger. Hunger is not limited to eating food. My hunger was for understanding, for touch, and for acceptance. My fear was not of success. It was one of acceptance. This fear is reflected in both the wayward son as well as the older son. Neither one knew what rightfully belonged to them because of their misperception of the true heart of their father.

In the parable of the prodigal son, it is revealed of his perception when he said, "Give me my share." The older brother's misperception is revealed in verse 29, "…but answered his father, 'Look! All these years I've been slaving for you and never disobeyed your orders. Yet you never gave me even a young goat so I could celebrate with my friends." Neither son realized that all that the father had was also theirs. I suggest that the father used wisdom by only giving the prodigal son just enough to allow him to go learn his lessons of life in wild living. This event gives evidence that God will allow you to experience times of trouble so that you can see for yourself just how good it really is in the Father's House. This was unlike the older brother, who meanwhile was too busy with chores and keeping to a set of rules in wait of a "someday" reward.

"Meanwhile, the older son was in the field. When he came near the house, he heard music and dancing. So he called one of the servants and asked him what was going on" (Luke 15:25-26) (NIV)

As Jesus spoke this parable to the scribes and Pharisees, He was also exposing their heart that was polluted with religion. Not only did it pollute their hearts, but religion had also caused a misperception of God as well as the storyteller himself, Jesus. As wonderful as the story is in revealing the heart of God and the powerful message of redemption, it also reveals just how blind people are who have been Christians their entire lives. They are like the scribes and Pharisees that Jesus was speaking to.

Let us now look at Galatians 4:1-7 from the NIV version of Scripture.

"What I am saying is that as long as the heir is underage, he is no different from a slave, although he owns the whole estate" (verse one).

What this verse revealed to me in my personal life was the fact that although I am a son of God and a rightful heir to the whole kingdom of God, I will never possess what is rightfully mine as long as I remain in immaturity.

"The heir is subject to guardians and trustees until the time set by his father" (verse two).

This event was the time set by the father where he would soon execute his will through the redemptive work of Calvary in his own begotten son Jesus. Through the work of redemption, He would make it possible to adopt many more sons into His family. Let me continue with scripture before I get ahead of myself. Oh, I feel the "preach" upon me!

"So also, when we were underage, we were in slavery under the elemental spiritual forces of the world" (verse three).

The same scripture in King James Version:

"Even so we, when we were children, were in bondage under the elements of the world."

God will allow you to experience times of trouble so that you can see for yourself just how good it really is in the Father's House.

These basic principles of the world speak of the "Law."

"But when the set time had fully come, God sent His Son, born of a woman, born under the law, to redeem those under the law, that we might receive adoption to sonship" (verses four and five).

Now is the time to preach! It was on the behalf of all of mankind that Jesus was born of a woman so that He could properly fulfill the demands of the law. The total passage of scripture here in Galatians 4:1-7 gives reason for maturity—for growth. The last part of verse 15 gives us the reason for growing up so that we may receive all that rightfully belongs to us.

Redemption is restoration. I had often heard this spoken many times throughout my life, but I never grasped the reality of it until I began to see myself as God saw me. My perception of myself was the hindering factor that kept me from enjoying life as a son. I had often stated that I had nothing to be restored. All I knew was that I had no desire to be restored to the life that I lived. I never realized my true position as a son. This self-evaluation only kept me thinking I had to do something to obtain a position.

My natural father was a very decisive man and was very strict in his disciplinary actions. I often viewed him as being angry with me. His facial expressions along with the tone of his voice would cause me to be overcome with fear of the punishment that was to come. It would take hours, even days for the fear and anger toward my dad to subside. It was in this time that I also would have to convince myself that dad would not be mad at me anymore. Please understand that I am not saying my dad was a mean man. I'm making a point to reveal how my perception of my dad was distorted and how this misperception caused me to miss out on what my dad really wanted for me.

I'm reminded of a time that I was experiencing a healthy sobriety when my father and my relationship began a mending process. It was a time that we began enjoying a father/son relationship. My mother asked me, "What did your daddy do?" "What do you mean?" I replied. She went on to say how there was a visible change in our relationship. I just smiled and said, "He didn't do anything. It was what I did that caused change." What I did was change my perception of who my father was and what he wanted for me to be—his son.

It was just recently that my father and mother had come to see me here at the Center of Hope. As I sat in the Sunday morning service, and the praise and worship team began worship, my father came to me and wrapped his arms around me and held me in his arms. I wept. I am now 52 years of age, and at that moment I felt the love of my father in a way that I longed for as a child. We limit ourselves to receive feelings of affirmation such as this one because of how we think others see us. If we don't see ourselves worthy, we will never experience the acceptance of the Father. The Father can only give you what you are able to receive.

In the story of the prodigal, we have failed to comprehend the true heart of the father who awaited the arrival of his son. The compassion of the father that was eager to restore all that he had upon his son seems incomprehensible by those like myself who felt unworthy of restoration. The relationship between my father and me has totally been restored, and I long to spend intimate time with him in our latter years. This relationship is the first to be restored in my life, and rightfully so. It takes precedence over all others. This holds true both spiritually and naturally. I do not worry anymore wondering if my relationship to my wife Kimberly or if my relationships to my daughters will be restored. I know deep in my heart that all will be restored when the time fully comes.

My acceptance as a son has become a reality in my life. I no longer sit in loneliness fantasizing about a someday reconciliation with my family. I remember countless times throughout my life where I would get lost in thought and dream of the time that I would be able to be re-united with my family and not feel like the "black sheep." This feeling of being the black sheep always made me feel less than or not measuring up to the standard that the other members of my family seemed to hold. In search of acceptance and approval, I became the family comedian. It seemed to work, but my reason was wrong. I still am the comedian, but it is for the sole purpose of creating a smile instead of receiving acceptance.

If you are reading this and find yourself in the shoes I once wore, let me say to you now, do not do what I did for the last forty plus years of my life—that is to hold on to a distorted view of what you perceive others to think of you, spiritually speaking. Do not let

Satan continue to talk to you into thinking that God expects you to measure up. He longs for your return so that he can lavish you with mercy and grace. He longs for you to call Him "Daddy." It is time to change our perspective of who He is. This change will take place the very moment you choose to believe. You must get out of the past and into the now, as there is no such place as a moment past. There are only moments present.

Our perception of God will determine the way we perceive ourselves. If you only see Him as "Master," you can only see yourself as a "servant." A servant seeks only a reward. A son receives an inheritance.

Galatians 4:5:

"...to redeem those under the law (slaves to sin), that we might receive adoption to sonship." (NIV)

These full rights that we are to receive are the inherited rights of being a son. It's called, *Sonship.* We receive this right through the spirit of adoption. The power of adoption is legal and binding. It is even more binding than natural birth and gives access to inheritance. I give witness to this as I adopted my oldest daughter, Ashley. I remember the day that I first laid eyes on her. She was around eleven months old and was as beautiful as a sunrise with golden locks of curls and big blue eyes. When our eyes met, she smiled and I melted. It was on this day, in that moment, that I experienced the overwhelming joy of being called "Daddy." This was the first word that she ever said to me as she pointed her little finger toward my chest as I held her in my arms. Oh, what I would give to have that moment again and know what I know now! I guess we all have made that statement at some point of time in our lives. I definitely would have done things differently in her and her sisters' lives. However, I can't change the past. I can only change the now.

Our perception of God will determine the way we perceive ourselves.

Remembering when I was in the lawyer's office to sign the adoption papers to receive Ashley as my own, the lawyers repeatedly questioned me, asking if I was sure that I wanted to go through with the adoption. Annoyed by their persistent questioning of my decision, I asked why they were doing so. Their answer was an explanation of the seriousness of adoption. They proceeded to tell me how by no means, whatsoever, that I could ever write her off. I could not adopt her to another man, forfeiting my rights as a father. I could in no way write her out of my will (if I had one!), nor could I stop her from receiving any inheritance (if any!). They also explained how the power of adoption was more legal and binding than that of the birth of my own offspring (children). They concluded by saying that I could give up my fatherly rights of my own offspring and exclude them from any will or inheritance, but in no way could I exclude Ashley. I agreed! When I signed the adoption papers, I was agreeing to the conditions and accepted her as my own, and she received my name. It was a choice I made, and I have never regretted it! My only regret was not remaining in her and her sisters' lives due to my self-centered and selfish lifestyle that was totally consumed and controlled by drugs and alcohol.

I, like the prodigal son who found himself feeding pigs, realized just how bad my life had gotten because of the bad decisions that I had made throughout my life. I still deal with the consequences of those decisions every day. However, I now deal with them with a sober mind and with an understanding that God is my Daddy and His desire is for me to not only be reconciled to Him, but also to my four beautiful daughters and all their children (my grandbabies) as well.

I was spiritually blind, and it was visibly seen by others. I had sacrificed everything in my life. I forfeited even my fatherly duties just to chase another high. As twisted as it seems, I didn't simply use drugs and alcohol just to get high; I used them to survive. It was what I had done to shut down my emotions of anger and guilt that were the result of my shame. Drugs and alcohol would temporarily hold my emotions at bay.

I suggest from personal experience that the prodigal son had a long journey home. Scripture does state that he headed for a distant land. This tells me he was far away. My journey home has taken me thirty-five years for the embrace of the Father (God) and the embrace of my Dad. The journey was worth it. Though someone may still be in their wilderness journey, it does not mean they do not long for home. I always longed for home, and on many accounts, I would be as close as simply pulling in the driveway only to drive away. The overwhelming of my emotions was what kept me away. I had to stay away to protect my family from me. Uncontrollable rages of anger always left a trail of destruction from broken doors to hurting others who were trying to help me. Trying to understand why I did the thing that I did, trust me when I say, serious cases need professional help, and you are not a professional!

Something as simple as a disgusting look can trigger a rage. An attempt to help can get you seriously hurt, both physically and emotionally. For this reason I would stay in a distant land with a distorted reason of justification of my absence of home. I have sacrificed more than I care to share; however, I now understand in full the words found in Hosea 6:6 (NIV):

"For I desire mercy, not sacrifice, and acknowledgment of God rather than burnt offerings."

The sacrifice that I gave was also revealed to me in verse 7:

"As at Adam, they have broken the covenant; they were unfaithful to me there."

I had broken covenant with God when, like Adam, I made a willful decision to disobey God. The result was a broken relationship. For this reason, I feel as to why I never stood fast in any other relationship, even with my own children.

I could never stand in a relationship because of the perception I had of God and of myself.

I could never stand in a relationship because of the perception I had of God and of myself. I only perceived Him as judgmental and required me to attain to a set of rules. I had heard of grace but never felt worthy of it. When I would see God's grace poured out on someone else, who I thought did not deserve it, I would become angry and jealous. Here is where I want to expose the heart of the older brother. This older brother's perception of his father was only of one who expected obedience and holding to a set of rules. He fulfilled these requirements, and it was made known in his speech with his father in Luke 15:29 (NIV):

> "But he answered his father, Look! All these years I've been slaving for you and never disobeyed your orders..."

The older son's perception of his father is what created his behavior. It also limited his father's ability to bless him. I have come to realize that God can only elevate you to the level of your understanding of who He is. What you believe determines what you will receive.

Not only does our belief system determine our actions, but it will also deprive you of any blessings that are in store for you.

Matthew 8:13:

"Then Jesus said to the centurion, 'Go! It will be done just as you believed it would.' And his servant was healed at that moment." (NIV)

I have come to realize that God can only elevate you to the level of your understanding of who He is.

What comes out of our mouths reveals what truly is in our hearts. The older brother's belief system was distorted and became a curse to him. He demeaned his father's character by accusing him of his inability to recognize his works and labors by not rewarding him with a young goat. He also saw his father as unfair by lavishing the younger brother with the restorative gifts of a New Covenant and blessing him with these gifts and then celebrating the return of his wayward son. This older brother was as blind as the scribes and Pharisees of whom Jesus was speaking. The true heart of God is a desire to bring sight to the blind—to those whose perception of him has been distorted by religious blindness.

In verse thirty-one, the father's response gave revelatory truth to his son and should do so to us as well.

"My son, the father said, 'you are always with me, and everything I have is yours.' "

There are many who suffer from religious blindness. They have been in the church all their lives and have missed out on all the blessings of God because they have been too busy working for God, and it has robbed them of experiencing a true intimate relationship with Him. I have found myself in both sons. They both have revealed to me two extreme sides of myself that needed balancing. By recognizing my imbalance created a need for change. I had to change my perspective of my father, both God in heaven as well as my dad here on earth. My distorted perception of both has robbed me of ever truly experiencing the joy of being a father to my own children. I simply did not know how to be a father, because I never allowed mine to be one to me.

The healing experience that I now have has come through this powerfully spoken parable known as "The Prodigal Son," by the greatest storyteller of all, Jesus. He has shown me the true heart of God and how much He loves me—unconditionally! It is time for our perspective view of God to change. Change is possible the moment you decide to believe.

The choice is yours.

Chapter Eight

THE BASEMENT

As we have explored the powerful parable of the prodigal son, we have discussed how both sons had the wrong perception of their father and how it also created a wrong perception of themselves. With this wrong perception (spiritual blindness), both sons had limited themselves to what rightfully belonged to them. One asked for what he thought was his share; the other son had full access, yet he possessed nothing. We also have discussed the heart of the father and what his desire for his sons was. That desire was that their lives be opened and to realize their true position as sons. They both had become spiritually blind, and their blindness created limits to their ability to receive. The parable ended with the father saying, "But we had to celebrate and be glad, because this brother of yours was dead and is alive again. He was lost and is found."

Although Jesus ended this parable of the prodigal (wayward) son, it was not the end of the story. As I have related to both sons in the parable, I have related much more to the wayward son. I would have to say that the return of the wayward son was but the beginning of the process of change in his life. Change is a process, and old habits and behaviors have a tendency to hang around just as a born again believer does not walk in complete maturity. He has to grow up.

I would have to suggest that the wayward son had developed some dependency on what I myself have dealt with in drugs and alcohol. These are physical dependencies, yet there are mental and emotional issues that also need attention. The emotions of guilt, remorse, and shame are not easily shaken, even after you have made a decision for change and have given yourself over to the care of God. I call those emotions *Basement Items.* They are what we have stored or suppressed down in the basement area of our soul. For me, I thought they no longer existed. They are still there stored away, asleep, resting for their opportunity to attack. I have often fallen for the deception of their silence.

When you make the decision to return home, your emotions will do one of two things:

1) They will bombard you in an attempt to keep you in your mess.
2) They will go to sleep, or silence themselves in wait for you to let your guard down.

In both cases they will attack you with guilt and an overwhelming sense of unworthiness in an attempt to cover you in shame. This mode of silence is dangerous when it silences itself. It becomes as a lioness that stalks its prey. She walks along the edges of the pathway home. Her eyes are upon you, and you catch glimpses of her through the tall grass and trees. You tell yourself that she is not real, and the fear of her attack momentarily subsides. The voice of your father lets you know you have arrived home.

As the father runs to you and throws himself on you, the emotions of the father triggers the attack. The attack of uncontrollable emotions begin to mangle and maul you just as a lioness to her prey. In these moments of uncontrollable emotions, friends (if any) and loved ones reach out to help but only get themselves entangled in the attack.

Through the years I learned how to recognize when my emotions were awakening and would begin to prepare myself for the attack. The attacks are unavoidable, and at times, unbearable. Other times I could hold off the attacks by use of drugs and alcohol (if available). At times nothing worked at all. My fear was always of being in public or around family when my attacks would occur. I could usually tell if my emotions were just taunting me, or if they were in attack mode. I was able to do so by the level of anger that

I would feel. If I got mad, I was okay. If I got angry, I began to prepare myself. If I began to experience rage, I stood no chance.

This is spiritual warfare, and most do not survive. This is what claimed my brother's life. He was tired and exhausted to the point that death seemed to be the only way for victory. The only way to protect those he loved was to put his emotions to death, and there is only one way to do so. Yes, there is only one way to put your emotions to death. However, our emotions do not have to be our enemy. Oftentimes my brother and I would end up in rehabilitation centers, mental hospitals, or jail due to the attacks of our emotions. There is no proof that the things that my brother and I dealt with would give evidence that they happened to the wayward son. I can only speak of my own personal experiences as I put my own conclusion to the parable of the wayward son.

> *The emotions of guilt, remorse, and shame are not easily shaken, even after you have made a decision for change and have given yourself over to the care of God.*

The wayward son was welcomed home with outstretched arms of the father. He was given total restoration of honor, authority, and position. The sealing of this new covenant was done before he ever made it completely home. As he and his father reached the house, the celebration began. As the party started and the festivities were in full swing, the sleeping emotions of the wayward son began to awaken to the sound of music. The memories of where he had been and what he had done began to overtake him. Such memories have a way of stealing your joy.

In an attempt to not spoil the moment of joy for his father, the son fades into the crowd and out the back door. For me it was "the basement." Tears would roll down my cheeks as the thought of, "if daddy only knew where I have been and what I have done, would he have still accepted me? Would he still give me such extravagant gifts?" Could it be possible that these are the thoughts that caused the wayward son to never be able to accept his rightful position as a son? The story does not tell; however, I know from experience that the possibility is there.

The basement was a living quarter that I always went to. I never felt worthy of living upstairs where the festivities were. Although I was in the house, I still wasn't home. My father also gives witness to this as he has stated on several occasions that he had pictures of me during holiday seasons that prove my statement. I became a basement dweller; it was where I would seclude myself away from everyone else. I would even attempt to be absent during regular times of supper. I would slip in and out of the basement to avoid contact with my family. I would even wait till late hours to go upstairs in search of something to eat. Mom would always make sure there would be something plated for me in the refrigerator. She always knew the condition I was in by the amount of food that I would or would not eat.

Although I speak of a literal basement area in my father's house, I also speak of the internal basement in my life. It is found in the inner man. That is where the real healing occurs, even though we may not recognize it. Our problems are not superficial. Our problems are in the nonobvious basement areas of our lives. It is where our emotions live. I have often said that "what is visible on the outside is a reflection of what is going on in the inside." I would have to say that there is a truth here, yet it determines on how good of an actor or pretender a person is. I was a professional pretender. To only deal with the obvious is superficial and is nothing more than a band aid. It is like trying to deal with sin by the law. It is but a band aid mentality. All it can do is cover up your "boo-boo" and has absolutely no healing power whatsoever. The emotions of guilt, remorse, and shame are not easily shaken, even after you have made a decision for change and have given yourself over to the care of God. When the prodigal son returned home, his salvation was secured.

The parable does not give evidence of the son's journey home, nor does it give evidence of how long his journey was. Once again, I speak only for myself when I say that my journey to wholeness has been a grueling thirty-six years, as I was seventeen years old when I left home. This is true both in the natural and spiritual. This journey turned into a wilderness survival course, and it wasn't done clean and sober. When I first began my journey, it felt more like a welcome to the jungle. Lace up your boot straps and be sure you have your rabbit's foot good luck charm, because you're going to need it. If you feel that this is you, please listen to me and know when I say that you do not have to journey alone. You do not have to go through a wilderness survival course.

Change is a necessity for living in the newness of life. What needs change is our thinking.

One thing I have now come to realize is my homecoming is not a grueling work mentality of what I can accomplish, but an understanding that Jesus Himself had already walked before me through the desert. His journey was my journey. His destination was my destination. My suicidal mentality was a longing for home. I did not know then that I had already died a death in the person of Jesus Christ. His death was my death. Jesus did not die so you would not have to. He died because you did have to die.

Change is a necessity for living in the newness of life. What needs change is our thinking. We all must die to be born again, but we do not have to be like Judas who hung himself or even like my brother who hung himself in prison. Jesus' hanging was our hanging. The choice is yours. You can die a death unto yourself or you can become identified in the Body of Jesus as He hung suspended on Calvary's Hill.

Healing of the emotions is a process. I do believe in miracles, and I do believe in instantaneous change. However, there is also a process for healing and wholeness. Many more than most have to be walked through this process of healing. This is where the church comes in play. It is the duty of the church to stretch forth the hand of ministry. There are many churches that still remain without an out-reach ministry and is reflected in the fact that they have no increase. Most of these churches have the same

---

I do believe in miracles, and I do believe in instantaneous change. However, there is also a process for healing and wholeness.

---

thirty people for the last thirty years. I have often seen and heard tell of how these churches have turned people away because they did not measure up to their standards. This disqualified them for membership and participation in any church functions.

My wife Kimberly was doing the secretarial work for a local church in Arkansas a few years ago. One day she came home crying and was very upset. When I asked her what was wrong, she explained how the church was having a children's fun day. She continued to say how the church members were turning children away and not letting them participate in the fun day festivities due to the fact that they were not members of the church. It's one thing to turn away an adult, but a child? I dropped my head in shame and asked my wife to resign her position.

I remember a time that I was awakened by the rising of the morning sun as its warmth would de-thaw me from my seemingly frozen sleep in my truck. As I began to regain function, I sat up in my truck seat and began to clear the windshield with my shirt sleeve. Across the road from where I sat was a small country church. I began to weep and asked God to once again forgive me for the mess I had made of my life. I longed to just feel His presence and decided to slip in the church doors and sit on the back pew. I would wait until I thought the preaching would start to avoid any conversation with church members. I was only wanting to just sit in reverence before I journeyed home. As I entered the church door, I could feel all eyes upon me. I just nodded my head as if I was saying "hello." I was dirty and evidently stunk because a gentleman came to me with a handkerchief over his mouth and asked me to leave.

It was just days ago as I sat in my room here at the Center of Hope and listened to the most heart breaking story I have ever heard tell. My friend and roommate told of how a church had refused him help in burying his infant daughter. I was heartbroken, and the anger that I have had in the past toward the church reared up its ugly head. When I speak of the church, I do not include every church. But, I do not exclude them either. I speak mainly toward the traditional, legalistic church. This story was told me on Thanksgiving Day, and he has given me permission to tell his story, and I do so in hopes that it will cause you to self-check your heart. This is what he said:

"My wife and I had been high on heroin for a long time, especially me. I had been arrested and was released on house arrest. I had some money put back but had been spending my savings on heroin. My wife had given birth to our beautiful little girl. We had previously had a miscarriage, and now our little girl had been born prematurely. Her immune system, along with her lungs, was not fully developed. She acquired pneumonia and died. I sought help from family for aid in funeral expenses, but no one would help me because of all the trouble I had caused due to my drug addiction. My wife's family was unable to help financially. Her grandfather had given my wife's own burial plot in the graveyard of their church so she could bury her daughter.

After my family had refused to help us, I took what money I had left, which was a little less than $800.00 and went to the funeral home seeking help. The funeral director gave no help at first and walked me to the door. Out of anger and hurt, I lashed out at him verbally and walked away. He then called me back and told me that the best he could do was to give me a casket for what money I had in my pocket. He also stated that I would still have to get someone to dig the grave and lower the casket in the ground."

As my friend was telling his story, my mind drifted back to the burial of my brother Brandon. I began to put dirt on his grave when my sister Donia began shoveling dirt on the casket as fast and furious as her small arms could go. She was angry and hurt, also.

My friend continued with his story by saying,

"I was now broke, not a penny to my name. I did have a casket, a plot, and a dead daughter. I still had no idea as what to do. Then I thought, surely the church that owned the graveyard would help! It was my wife's church, even though she had not been attending. As I walked in the church with a sense of relief that my daughter will be buried, what hope I did have was shattered when the preacher refused to help me. He then told me, 'You're just gonna have to dig your own grave!' After I told him how I felt, I went and got me a shovel, a pick, and a rock bar and started digging. Have you ever had to dig Alabama red rock dirt? I dug for half a day and only had about a foot dug. The preacher, along with other members of the church, just watched as I poured sweat from my body as I labored digging. I would dig awhile and cuss God awhile. I would dig awhile; I would cry awhile. My wife came to help me, but she nearly had an emotional breakdown, and I made her leave. Truth be known, we were in an emotional breakdown. As I cried out to God asking why he was doing this to me, an elderly man in a suit and tie came to me and said, 'I have seen many things in my life, and I have lived a long time, but this is a first for me.' Then he took off his coat and tie, rolled up his sleeves and said, 'Throw me that rock bar, son. We have a grave to dig.' I never saw him again.

I apologized to my friend for the conduct of that church.

I remember the time when I found myself face down in a mud hole on the banks of the Mississippi River. Unable to get up, I couldn't even roll over. All I could do was raise my head out of the water just long enough to breathe before I would slowly drop back down into the muddy water to rest my neck. I was in a drunken stupor along with a broken back. I, like my friend, though our stories differ, were both broken and our emotions were damaged. We needed help, but it was nowhere to be found—not even a church would lend a helping hand.

I could not seem to connect to the church that I attended periodically, and I never really knew why. The pastor was powerful in executing his sermons. The praise team was the best of anywhere I have been, but when my life was in trouble, there was not even a phone call to see if I was okay. I'm not saying church is bad, and I'm not saying there are no churches that will not stretch out the hand of ministry to help you. I do say that the traditional church as a whole is as emotionally damaged as those of us who have turned to them for help. The church is in need of a healing itself.

I do not feel that it is the will of God for another generation to die from the crippling effects of the church. Looking into the book of Matthew, chapter 9, verses 18-26, the account of Jesus healing a sick woman on His way to raise a dead girl gives evidence of my claim. The story tells of Jesus being on His way to raise a dead girl when there was a woman who had an issue of blood for twelve years and needed healing. Woman is symbolic of the church. The bleeding issue expresses a crippling ministry, and the length of time (12 years) has a numerable meaning of government. I suggest this government to be reflective of the old Mosaic system or government of "The Law." The traditional, legalistic law-based church has had (still does) a crippling effect on people as seen here in Matthew 9.

"Jesus turned and saw her, 'take heart, my daughter,' He said, 'your faith has healed you,' and the woman was healed in that moment." (Matthew 9:22, NIV).

Notice here what Jesus spoke to her, "Take heart." This is where Jesus ministered to her emotions. This is where the Holy Spirit entered into her basement of emotions, as the heart is our basement. It is where the real healing takes place. It is where we have become crippled and bleeding. The issue of blood that the woman suffered was a bleeding heart. If it were an issue of blood that was obviously seen, she would have not been allowed to even be among the crowd under Jewish Law. If she would have been bleeding superficially in a manner in which most perceive her to have had, then she would have never been allowed in the synagogue. Scripture tells that she had been in the Temple and from doctor to doctor and had spent her entire inheritance in search of healing. Her broken bleeding heart could only be healed by "a touch."

In Ephesians, the Apostle Paul prayed that the eyes of our hearts be opened. He was praying that we come into an understanding that the heart's desire of the father (God) was to heal our broken hearts that are a result of our damaged emotions. This understanding does not come by intellectual knowledge that only deals with the superficial man. It comes only by the touch of grace. Our hearts are where the Holy Spirit seeks to reside. God is not concerned with the obvious external areas of our lives that are ruled by performance.

Ephesians 3:16-21

"I pray that out of his glorious riches he may strengthen you with power through his spirit in the inner being. So that Christ may dwell in your hearts through faith and I pray that you, being rooted and established in love, may have the power together with all the saints, to grasp how wide and long and high and deep is the love of Christ and to know this love that surpasses all knowledge (head knowledge) that you may be filled to the measure of the fullness of God. Now to him who is able to do immeasurably more than all we ask or imagine, according to his power that is at work within us (basement areas) to him be glory in the church and in Christ throughout all generations forever and ever!" (NIV)

For this reason Jesus had to stop and heal the crippled, bleeding heart of the church before he raises another generation. Scripture also says that the older women will teach the younger women. I don't understand how the church has remained so crippled and powerless and still claim to know the truth.

I have now come to realize that the reason that I have never experienced wholeness is because I was only seeking a visible, obvious change, never realizing how wounded I was in the inner man. Wholeness comes when the grace of God through the Holy Spirit heals us from the inside out. Real change begins when we exchange our broken lives for the life of Christ. In this moment of exchange, our emotions cease to control us. My wounded emotions were the cause of my problems but were the reason for this book.

> *Real change begins when we exchange our broken lives for the life of Christ.*

I began my book with Luke 4:18-19.

"...and to proclaim freedom for the prisoner [basement dwellers] and recovery of sight to the blind [spiritually blind]..."

When the eyes of our hearts are opened, our hearts are healed. Our emotions cease to rule over us, thereby, allowing our perspective of our father to no longer be tainted with the sense of unworthiness, shame, or guilt.

Allow the change to take place in the basement areas of your life. Don't let your damaged emotions keep you from enjoying what rightfully belongs to you. After all, the inheritance—all of it—belongs to you.

The decision is yours!

I have now come to realize that I have never experienced wholeness is because I was only seeking a visible, obvious change, never realizing how wounded I was in the inner man.

Chapter Nine

BORN BLIND

"...He sent me to proclaim freedom for the prisoners and recovery of sight for the blind..."

Restoring sight to the blind brings healing to our emotions. With this now restored vision, we can begin to see how our emotions were damaged. This is a hard chapter to write, as it causes me to also see where I have allowed the events of my past to not only rob me of my time with my family, but it has also robbed my family from time with me— especially my children and grandchildren. I know now how easy it is for children to misunderstand their parent(s)' actions, especially when their parent (me) was acting out of immaturity. I did not know how to be a daddy because I never allowed my dad to be a daddy to me. I often misunderstood him, and my perception of him became distorted. With this distorted perception of my dad, I had a low sense of self-worth and felt like I could never please him. This was the beginning of my emotional damage. I can only imagine how much emotional damage I have caused for my four daughters.

I have allowed the events of my past to not only rob me of my time with my family, but it has also robbed my family of time with me—especially my children and grandchildren.

When we suffer from emotional damage, it is hard to believe that healing would come by the eyes of our heart being opened. When one's heart has been broken, it is next to impossible to let your guard down and allow anyone to speak a word of truth into your life. The truth spoken is that if you desire healing of your damaged emotions, you're going to have to allow someone to help you. We must experience restoration of sight if we are to walk in wholeness.

I want to make a public confession. I have failed as a father to my girls. To them I dedicate this chapter of my book. To Ashley, Autumn, Kandis, and Anna, please forgive me for not being there for you as you grew up. There is no child that deserves to have to grow up without a dad. I can only imagine how much you felt rejected. For anyone who is reading this book, please know that I am not attempting to dig up old memories that bring you to a place of blame.
I only want to be able to use my own life's lessons to bring healing to damaged emotions and broken hearts. This can only be accomplished by the recovering of sight to the blind.

> *I did not know how to be a daddy because I never allowed my dad to be a daddy to me.*

I want to take a moment and pray that the eyes of our hearts be open and receptive as we travel through this chapter that I entitled, "Born Blind." To recover sight to the blind gives evidence that you once had sight. On the other hand, many have been born blind. Let us now go to John chapter nine.

"As he went along, he saw a man blind from birth. His disciples asked him, 'Rabbi, who sinned, this man or his parents that he was born blind?' 'Neither this man nor his parents have sinned,' said Jesus, 'but this happened so that the work of God might be displayed in his life.' " (John 9:1-3, NIV)

Before we go any further know that there is a high possibility that old memories will begin to surface, and sleeping emotions will begin to be awakened. Do not resist these awakening emotions for the fact that if you "don't deal with it, God can't heal it." As we begin to recover or receive sight, our emotions will not just give up their control. As we wrestle with the events of our past, we will also be tempted to handle them in the same old ways that we always have. We may seek to find someone or something to blame. As I have stated, I do not wish to play the blame game any longer. My new freedom that I have has only come by the grace of God that has empowered me with the ability to forgive others and mainly myself.

If we revert to blaming, our efforts for change will be counterproductive. Jesus went on to say that it was neither the man born blind nor his parents that had sinned. He stated that it was so God could be displayed in his life. Sometimes our mess is not because we sinned. Our mess is a result of a bad decision; or for some, their mess is because of someone else's bad decision. My daughters did not do anything to deserve the mess they experienced because of my inability to make good decisions. My prayer is that God be revealed to them as He was revealed to the man born blind, and also unto me. I pray that His power be displayed in their lives in such a mighty way that people who know them will not recognize them because of the work of God that will be displayed in their lives.

My new freedom that I have has only come by the grace of God that has empowered me with the ability to forgive others and mainly myself.

When I asked God to open my eyes, He sent me here to the Center of Hope. It was a more modern approach than making mud balls with spit and telling me to go wash the dirt out of my eyes. Wow! I just got a revelation (smiling)! My Siloam, the place where I have washed the dirt out of my eyes has been here at the Center of Hope discipleship program. It is where I have come to have my sight restored, when I had become blinded by the dirt in my life. Through my situations and circumstances, I had brought blindness upon myself by operating out of a spirit of unforgiveness and by attempting to handle my circumstances on my own. I did not seek help from others or God for the simple fact that I was angry with both. As I read John chapter nine, I realized that my circumstances, though they were a result of bad decisions, were also evidence of God being displayed in my life. Romans 8:28 came to reality in my life as God was bringing all things together for the good of His purpose in my life. As I now look back, I see that I have lost nothing. God simply removed everything out of my life so that I had nothing nor no one that I could turn to as a resource.

For the first time in my life my eyes are wide open without the help of methamphetamines. It is only by the power of His Holy Spirit that now lives and has His way in my life. I now live in a healthy lifestyle, both spiritually and naturally. I am no longer controlled by my emotions. Giving or receiving forgiveness can both be hard to do because of built-up anger toward others and yourself.

If we revert to blaming, our efforts for change will be counterproductive.

Matthew 18:21-22

"Then Peter came and asked, 'Lord, how many times shall I forgive my brothers when he sins against me? Up to seven times?' " (NIV)

Here we see where Peter asked the Lord how many times he should forgive his brother when he sins against him. Before Jesus could answer, Peter made the suggestion that seven times should be sufficient. Jesus answered with a statement of "not seven, but seventy times seven times. "Seventy times seven" is figurative of an unlimited number. Forgiveness of others was always easy for me once my anger subsided. Asking for forgiveness wasn't as easy to do. Asking God for forgiveness was even difficult at times, but God forbid (figure of speech) if I was to forgive myself. Just as the principle of love is defined in Matthew 22:37-39 with verse 39 being the key—"love your neighbor as yourself." Forgiveness also operates from this same principle. Problem is that this just might be what we have been doing. It just may be that if we don't love ourselves, then we cannot forgive ourselves. You can only give what you have first received. I know this sounds paradoxical to where scripture says that it's better to give than to receive, yet we have to understand that most people are dysfunctional in some area or another in their lives.

Giving or receiving forgiveness can both be hard to do because of built-up anger toward others and yourself.

The strength of a chain is only as strong as its weakest link, a catch phrase that gives revelatory truth concerning the system of our mind. My brother often would ask me to help him help someone else. My answer was always, "Help you help them? We can't even help ourselves!" You couldn't make one good man out of us both. Forgiveness is the same way. You cannot forgive others until you learn how to forgive and accept forgiveness of yourself.

When we explore our inner healing, we will come to understand that the majority of our fears come from a sense of unworthiness, low self-esteem, and the feeling of not being loved. I once stated that my brother was an egotistical maniac with an inferiority complex. Now that's a recipe for disaster! Only problem was, I was no different. Have you ever noticed how the very thing that disgusts you in someone else is usually the very thing that reminds you of you? Everyone does this either consciously or unconsciously. We all do it, and we are quick to point it out to them or others. Self-esteem and self-worth are powerful healing agents for our broken hearts and damaged emotions. Self-esteem and self-worth comes only when we get a revelation of Jesus and the work of redemption—called grace!

I John 4:10-16 (NIV)

"This is love; not that we loved God, but that he loved us and sent his son as an atoning sacrifice for our sins. Dear

---

The majority of our fears come from a sense of unworthiness, low self-esteem, and the feeling of not being loved.

---

friends, since God so loved us, we ought to love one another. No one has ever seen God; but if we love one another, God lives in us and his love is made complete (displayed) in us. We know that we live in him and he in us, because he has given us of his spirit. And we have seen and testify that the Father has sent his Son to be the savior of the world."

To know this kind of love creates respect for yourself and others. The scripture that says, "It's better to give than receive," is without question, absolutely true! I have never experienced more pleasure in my life than I do now when I see the truth of God setting people free from the bondage of self that once bound me. You must understand that when dealing with emotionally damaged people, chances are that they will hurt you. Don't stop helping them as the reward of giving becomes far greater than the ability to receive. It's when our eyes become opened from being spiritually blind—or "born blind." You have to learn how to be loved as well as be love.

I have never experienced more pleasure in my life than I do now when I see the truth of God setting people free from the bondage of self that once bound me.

Again, you cannot give what you don't have. The restoring process that takes place, as our eyes begin to open, has a tendency to create fear. This fear of the unknown does subside as the eyes of our understanding begin to open, and we know that we are being taken care of by the indwelling of the Holy Spirit.

II Timothy 1:7

"For God hath not give us a spirit of fear; but of power, of love and of a sound mind."(KJV)

From the NIV version, it states that "God did not give us a spirit of timidity, but a spirit of power, of love, and of self-discipline." Self-discipline comes when we begin to allow our emotions to heal. It is when we control our emotions instead of our emotions controlling us. Fear is what always motivated my anger. Whenever I felt threatened, fear would always overtake me.

I am again reminded of a childhood event that gives evidence to my claim. I was in the second grade—maybe third grade— when two African-American boys would always want my lunch money. Fear of what would seem to be the result if I didn't pay up would always cause me to hand over my quarter. A quarter a day to keep from getting beat up seemed to be the thing to do until hunger set in. As I stated in a previous chapter, hunger has a way of causing a person to re-think a situation. I had to come up with a new plan, and that I did. I figured that if I didn't pay the quarter, then I could skip the bus ride and just run home. I only lived a couple of blocks from the school, anyway. This worked fine for a day or two until the McVey brothers figured out my scheme. Then it became a daily foot race around the playground, behind the cafeteria, down the straight stretch along side of the chain link fence, and a side slide under the loose end of the fence like a baseball player sliding into home base. Once free from the schoolyard, I had a beaten trail between the neighborhood houses and into the front yard of home. If I was quick enough, I could reach the front porch where I would dance a jig of victory as I entered the screen door. Other times, I barely made it into the yard where a big oak tree stood. It served as a refuge in times of trouble. Then there were times that I didn't make it home. Black eyes and bloody noses gave evidence of my troubles.

One particular day I had a smile on my face as I had a reasonable distance between me and the McVey brothers. As I entered the front yard in full stride, I saw my dad standing on the front porch with a belt in hand. I had a choice to make—turn and face the McVey brothers or face the belt. I chose the McVey brothers. When I say fear motivates anger, I mean every word of it. I fought for my life, and won. I had battle scars, but they seemed to be easier to deal with than the wrath of the belt.

Fear is a motivator; however, it does not have to motivate anger. Fear is an emotion that is often misused and does not have to promote hostility. Healthy fear is a respect. As I was growing up, I had developed a fear of God as in "scared," due to the fact that I had only associated fear with being scared. One of the best descriptions of fear that promoted hostility is found in I Samuel chapter 18. So much can be spoken of in chapter 19, such as jealousy, fear, respect, loyalty and the birthing of a covenant of friendship. For now, I want to stay on the subject of fear, and it is first cousin to hostility. Both were expressed through the life of King Saul. His anger toward David began when they returned from battle and the women came out to meet them singing praises to David, saying, "Saul has slain his thousands, and David his tens of thousands" (I Samuel 18:7). Verse 8 states that Saul became very angry. It was the birthing of a jealous anger that fueled hostility until his death.

As I read this passage of scripture that tells of Saul's jealousy toward David, I began to realize how we become role players. I have to relate these roles to myself as I have dealt with such roles as David, who became a victim, to the role of Saul, who was the abuser. Not only have I dealt with abuse, but I realize that I have also abused others (not sexually). My abuse to others was a mental and emotional abuse that was unintentional. It is something that automatically happens when a person such as myself lives a dysfunctional lifestyle. Those that get abused become victims of circumstance. These are those who fall into the role of being a martyr. In my case the martyrs were all my family members, as they all have suffered on my behalf in my cry for help.

My abuse to others was a mental and emotional abuse that was unintentional. It is something that automatically happens when a person such as myself lives a dysfunctional lifestyle.

My petition to God was much like the petition of Rahab to the spies when they went into Jericho.

Joshua 2:13

"That you will spare the lives of my father and mother, my brothers and sisters, and all who belong to them—and that you save us from death." (NIV)

Something struck me funny when I began reading this account of the spies that Joshua sent into Jericho. Of all the places the spies could have gone to, I wonder why they picked Rahab's house. Rahab was a prostitute, and prostitutes had ways to let the public know when the door was open for business. I better leave this be (smiling really big!). Let me say that it doesn't matter what the spies' motives were (if any) for picking Rahab's house to enter.

What mattered was that she spared their lives and aided in their safety. The end result was that she became a woman of great faith, and she stands among the greatest of those like Abel, Enoch, Noah, Abraham, Isaac, Jacob, Joseph, and Moses.

Hebrews 11:30-31 (NIV)

"By faith the walls of Jericho fell...By faith the prostitute Rahab, because she welcomed the spies, was not killed with those who were disobedient."

It was also through the lineage of Rahab that Jesus Himself was born.

There is a powerful display of the benefits of risking change found in the story of Rahab the prostitute in chapter two of the Book of Joshua—a change from prostitution to becoming a woman with such faith that she stands among the giants of faith listed in Hebrews 11. We are no different. We have all been guilty of prostituting our purpose by settling for the lie that says change is impossible. It does not matter where we have been or what we have done, the Father waits for us to return so that He can restore our sight or even give us sight so that we can see ourselves the way He sees us.

We need not be afraid of new beginnings. God has always used common, ordinary dysfunctional people such as myself so that He can be displayed. All we are required to do is to be willing to change.

Change is possible, and the choice is still yours!

Chapter Ten

THE DEATH SENTENCE

Now that we have entered into the basement areas of our lives (our souls), we can then begin to rid ourselves of the unhealthy emotions of jealousy, envy, anger, strife, guilt, shame, remorse, judgmentalism, bitterness, and ungratefulness—to name a few. Chances are that you will experience the feelings of emptiness and loneliness. Please do not allow them to cause you to seek the quick fixes of drugs and alcohol abuse. Do not seek a quick fix of entering into a relationship with another person other than Jesus Christ Himself. It is only in Him that we will ever be able to fill such voids in our lives.

It has only been about six months ago that I had found myself once again with no one in my life. I was all alone and lonely. When one comes to this place in their lives, they seem to have a tendency to go into survival mode instead of to God. Survival mode can only keep you alive to an old nature of sin struggling through life. Survival mode is when a person is totally dependent on human reasoning and the basic principles of the world. This world that I speak of is of an old world or nature that is governed by a set of rules and regulations known as The Law. We need only to depend on the power of grace. We need to depend on Christ and the finished work of redemption that He completed in us (not for us) on Calvary's Hill. Loneliness can be a good thing if it causes you to turn to God instead of from God. Without God, a person can and will remain in a constant state of loneliness even when there are others in their lives. In my case, I was lonely and alone. I was to the point that I gave up hope of ever experiencing permanent fulfillment.

I had just experienced ten years of enjoying what I thought to be a perfect world. My wife and I lived in a small country home with a garden in the backyard that I attended to daily. We both had good jobs, and both owned our own vehicles. You might ask, "Isn't this normal?" I guess it would be if you are normal. I wasn't. It was the first time in my life that I actually held a job other than being self-employed. It was the first time in my life that I actually lived at the same address for an extended time where I received my mail. It was the first time in my life that I actually experienced the joy of being a husband. I even felt loved by my wife. We never argued, not one time for a period of around seven years. I could walk less than 100 yards from my front porch and be in the best crappie fishing in the state of Arkansas. I could drive two miles down the road and be in the best coon hunting in the United States. I lived in a fairy tale world, and it was good! The only problem was that I had become complacent in my spiritual life. I would quickly tell someone how blessed I was and how God had provided for me. I had acquired more material possessions than I ever had before in my life. I had trucks, boats, a camper, good coonhounds, riding lawnmowers, etc. God did bless me with them as well as with my job and my wife. God wants to bless you with these things when you keep Him first in your life. I was very comfortable in the way I was living.

Loneliness can be a good thing if it cause you to turn to God instead of from God.

Let me say that there is nothing wrong with living a good country life, and I look forward to doing so again. My problem was that my wife, my home, and everything attached to them became my god. Scripture tells us that God does not want us to have any other god before Him. My little paradise is what I lived for, and the comfort of home began to invade and replace church on Sundays. The joy of fishing and hunting interrupted my God-time. My Bible began to collect dust, and my chair-side table no longer had study books on it. My study books were replaced by crappie jigs and coonhound magazines.

Before I could realize what I was doing, the drugs and alcohol had re-entered my life. The world as I knew it began to crumble. My wife and I both lost our jobs, our vehicles were breaking down, my dog died, I broke my back, and my aorta collapsed. I was diagnosed with Type II diabetes and arthritis, and the list goes on and on. I began blaming God for the hell I was experiencing. My sleeping emotions began to awaken after a ten-year nap. They became fuel for my anger and were my only companions. Problem was my emotions were as much of a mess as I was.

As I mentioned earlier in this chapter, loneliness can be beneficial. This is where my loneliness benefited me. My loneliness had brought me to a position of decision. I had to make a decision for change. I had to rid myself of pride and ask for help from the one I was angry with—God. Colossians 1:21-22 became a present reality as I felt that I had become alienated from God Himself because of anger toward Him. I had become hostile in thought as I was experiencing homicidal and suicidal thoughts, and I was engaged in the sinful activity of drug and alcohol use and abuse.

My loneliness had brought me to a position of decision. I had to make a decision for change.

When I felt that God was against me and not for me, I would become more hostile as I got higher and higher on meth. It was as if I was trying to prove to God that "I got this!" And I needed no help from Him. As I look back at this moment of my life, I can now see how He was ever present in my mess and was ever working in me the ministry of reconciliation. Despite of how I felt toward Him, and despite of what I was doing, He kept me from harming others and myself. In the midst of it all, He revealed to me what was true of me. He began to show me who I really was by revealing Jesus to me. He showed me the message of the cross. It was the revelation of redemption.

> Let us look now at Colossians 1:21-22 [brackets are mine for emphasis].

> "Once you were alienated from God and were enemies in your minds [thoughts] because of your evil behavior. But now He has reconciled you by Christ's physical body through death to present you holy in his sight, without blemish and free from accusation—" (NIV)

You see, it's not what we do or what we have already done, but it's what God has done in the work of redemption through His only begotten Son, Jesus, which reconciles us. We were only enemies in our minds (thoughts). Let me say once again that when we begin to see ourselves the way God sees us, then we will change the way we think and begin to live a victorious Christian life.

You see, it's not what we do or what we have already done, but it's what God has done in the work of redemption through His only begotten Son, Jesus, which reconciles us.

Satan can no longer accuse you before God. Actually, he hasn't been able to do so since Christ stripped Him of his power through the death sentence that was executed on the cross. It states plainly in this passage of scripture that God has (past tense) reconciled us unto Himself by Christ's physical body through death. The death sentence was executed, and we died our second death. Satan lost his power over death, and he no longer has reign in our life. Satan knows this to be true; he just doesn't want you to know this to be true. His only weapon is you. If he can keep you in ignorance of what God says is true of you, then he can keep you alienated from God through the mind. I call it "stinkin'-thinkin.'"

The most quoted memory verse here at the Center of Hope discipleship program is II Corinthians 5:17:

"Therefore, if anyone is in Christ, the new creation has come: The old has gone, the new is here." (NIV)

It may be the most quoted because of the fact that it is easy reading and easy to remember. I also feel that most who quote this verse do not realize the powerful concept that everything really is new. I myself have been guilty of the same. It wasn't until I continued reading in chapter 5 that I grabbed ahold of this powerful truth. Then, II Corinthians 5:18 goes on to say:

"All this is from God, who reconciled us to himself through Christ and gave us the ministry of reconciliation." (NIV)

God has given to us the ministry of reconciliation. We do not earn it through good behavior. We only receive it as a gift from God. However, we can only receive to the degree that we believe.

Let's keep reading—II Corinthians 5:19:

"That God was reconciling the world to himself in Christ, not counting people's sins against them. And he has committed to us the message of reconciliation." (NIV)

God does not keep record of your wrongs as He does not count men's sins against them. God only keeps record of the righteousness of Himself in Christ.

Romans 5:18-19:

"Here it is in a nutshell: Just as one person did it wrong and got us in all this trouble with sin and death, another person did it right and got us out of it. But more than just getting us out of trouble, he got us into life! One man said no to God and put many people in the wrong; one man said yes to God and put many in the right." (MSG)

As born again New Covenant believers, God no longer keeps record of your wrongs. This is evident in the Book of Hebrews in chapter eleven that is called "The Hall of Faith." Nowhere is there mention of the wrong that was in the lives of those listed as the patriarchs of faith. It only speaks of their faith and how righteousness was imputed unto them. Abraham himself was and still is considered to be the Father of Faith; yet, nowhere in the New Testament does it speak of him being a liar when he said that his wife was his sister in order to save their lives in Egypt. Nowhere in the list of these faith giants does it mention their past mistakes and failures. It only speaks of their faith.

If we look at Abraham and God's promise to him in Hebrews 11:12, it says:

"And so from this one man, and he as good as dead, came descendants as numerous as the stars in the sky and as countless as the sand on the seashore." (NIV)

Does this sound like God kept record of his wrongs? This is also a remarkable parallel to Christ Himself as the one who tasted death for everyone.

II Corinthians 5:21

"God made him who had no sin to be sin for us, so that in him we might become the righteousness of God." (NIV)

Let us also look at II Corinthians 5:21 from The Message Bible (MSG):

"How? You ask. In Christ, God put the wrong on him who never did anything wrong, so we could be put right with God."

God's will was being done in my life despite what I was doing and without my permission. He was not keeping record of my wrong. He was revealing to me of my rights. I often thought that I had to do something right in order to qualify myself for redemption. If this is you, let me say that it is not true! I thought that if I could be in the right revival, under the right preacher, in a feel-good moment, then maybe God would consider me worth saving.

In the meantime, I would dig deep into scripture, pray harder, go to church, and pay my tithes in an attempt to gain favor. It never happened! Please know that I'm not saying reading your Bible and praying is wrong, and that it is not beneficial, as it is what keeps Jesus and His work of redemption the central focus of my life. There are benefits in doing so, but they should not be done with a works-based mentality with an expectation of a reward of intimacy or favor. Reading, praying, going to church and paying your tithes should be a result of intimacy with Him.

It was just this past Wednesday night that Gary Burns, our senior pastor and overseer here at the Center of Hope, delivered a prophetic word to prove my claim in his message entitled, "The Power of Grace." He used the illustration of the difference between being pardoned and paroled. When a crime has been committed and a judgment has been passed, the one who committed the crime begins to serve his sentence. During a time of his sentencing comes a possibility of a parole. A parole is based on good behavior, and if given a parole, he is released from his incarcerations. If for any reason his probation becomes violated by bad behavior, he then is re-incarcerated. Either way, he is still under penalty of the law and the punishment of his crime. When a person is pardoned, he is completely set free from the punishment of his crime and his slate is wiped clean. All record of wrong has been removed and is as the offense never took place. When we look at this from a spiritual viewpoint, there is no better book than the book of Hebrews that gives evidence of our rights.

I suggest reading the entire fifth chapter. Let us look at Romans 5:16 from the Message Bible:

"There is no comparison between that death-dealing sin and this generous, life-giving gift. The verdict on that one sin was the death sentence; the verdict on the many sins that followed was this wonderful life sentence." (MSG)

This makes me shout every time I read it!

Follow me now as I attempt to unfold my thoughts. The death sentence was issued to everyone including you and me. It was issued unto us through the disobedience of the one man, Adam. For it is in the nature of Adam that we all became sinners and subject to death. Scripture says that the many sins that followed were issued the verdict of life. However, we need to know that you cannot receive a new life until you understand the principle of being "born again."

You cannot be born again unless you first die a "second death." Let me remind you that we are not speaking of a natural death. We are speaking of a spiritual death. This gives reason for the cross and its work of redemption. Many times I have heard it said that Christ died so that we would not have to. This, also, is not true. The truth is Christ died because we had to die in order to be born again.

Death was the penalty of our sins. Matthew 24:1-35 gives a powerful description for the cause of Christ on your behalf. It gives reason for the "death sentence." We have all died in Christ— all as unto those who come to understand who they are in Him. We all have to die a second death. We can do one of two things: we can die a death unto ourselves, and that will be the end of it; or, we can identify with who we are in Him (Christ). His death then becomes our death. Either way, we die.

The truth is Christ died because we had to die in order to be born again.

The Apostle Paul stated in Romans chapter 7, verses 24-25:

"What a wretched man I am! Who will rescue me from this body that is subject to death? Thanks be to God, who delivers me through Jesus Christ our Lord." (NIV)

When we look at the cross we also see two thieves hanging with Jesus. One recognized Jesus and identified himself in Him, and he entered into paradise "on that day."

John 14:20-21:

"On that day you will realize that I am in my Father, and you are in me, and I am in you. Whoever has my commands and keeps them is the one who loves me. The one who loves me will be loved by my Father, and I too will love him and show myself to them." (NIV)

The other thief spoke selfishly unto Jesus by saying, "Aren't you the Christ? Save yourself and us!" (Luke 23:39). Then the one said, "Don't you fear (respect) God, since you are under the same sentence?" (Luke 23:40). This sentence that he was speaking of was the "death sentence." He continued in verse 41, saying, "We are punished justly, for we are getting what we deserve..." It was at this moment that Jesus was drawing all men unto Himself.

To die one death for all, the one thief—as with Jesus—who had betrayed him died a death unto himself. If they could have held on for a few more hours, Jesus' death would have also been their death, and they too would be with Him in paradise. They could have then identified in Christ's death and received eternal life. Please do not sell yourself short of this powerful truth. You do not have to die a death unto yourself. You can identify in Christ's death and receive the "life sentence" that is issued unto the many sins that followed the one.

The Apostle Paul struggled with this reality and is described in Romans 7:7-25. When I began reading this passage of scripture, I began to see me. I, like Paul, suffered from analytical paralysis. Paul could not help being analytical, as he was once a scribe of scribes. He had to have an answer for everything until he was delivered from his body of death—his old man that he was as Saul. Myself, I psychoanalyzed everything! It was also what kept me spiritually handicapped. I was in as much of a mess as a crippled coon with a hell hound on his trail. I had a full-blown case of analytical paralysis. I analyzed until I became paralyzed (smile).

Romans 7:18

"For I know that good itself does not dwell in me, that is, in my sinful nature.[a] For I have the desire to do what is good, but I cannot carry it out." (NIV)

I psychoanalyzed everything! It was also what kept me spiritually handicapped. I was in as much of a mess as a crippled coon with a hell hound on his trail!

This scripture as most scriptures has been misinterpreted. Many seem to quote it as saying, "Nothing good lives in me." This is not what Paul said. He said, "...that is, in my sinful nature." He was speaking of his old nature of sin, not in his new nature in Christ. Paul also said that the old man (old nature) that he was, was dead.

II Corinthians 5:17:

"Therefore, if anyone is in Christ, the new creation has come. The old has gone, the new is here." (NIV)

You may ask, "If the old man is dead, then why do we still battle with sin?" My answer is that although our old nature is dead and gone, our flesh is ever present and alive. When Adam was created, he was created in God's likeness and in His image. God is a spirit being, and so likewise was Adam. He then was placed into bodily form.

Genesis 2:7

"Then the Lord God formed a man[a] from the dust of the ground and breathed into his nostrils the breath of life, and the man became a living being." (NIV)

We are also spirit beings and inhabit a human body. Many seem to think the opposite. They believe that we are human beings that are in search of a spiritual habitation. This is not how God designed it to be. When Adam disobeyed God by eating from the tree of knowledge, his spirit (or the life of God) was removed from him and he died. He died spiritually, and we all have felt the sting of this death.

I Corinthians 15:56-57

"The sting of death is sin, and the power of sin is the law. But thanks be to God! He gives us the victory through our Lord Jesus Christ." (NIV)

Paul had also stated just prior to this that death had been swallowed up in victory (I Corinthians 15:54-55).

"...death has been swallowed up in victory. Where O death is your victory? Where O death is your sting? "

It is for the purpose of victory that a second death is required. We have to allow ourselves to die to an old lifestyle with old habits and beliefs in order to experience being born again. We cannot do this on our own! It will not change you! We can only do so through identifying in the death of Jesus. You can hate your circumstances and situations all you want to, but it will not change you. There is a saying here at the Center of Hope Discipleship Program that is often quoted when a student seems to think, "I got this!" It is, "If you could have changed yourself, you would have already done it, and you would not be here."

I pray that you do not do as I have in my past and perceive the principle of death the wrong way and try to die a death unto yourself. Let me remind you that we are speaking of a spiritual death and not that of a natural death. If we die in the natural, we die a physical death, and it's over, period! The spirit man has to have a physical body in which to live in order for God's glory to be seen on earth.

I Corinthians 15:51-52

"Listen, I tell you a mystery; We will not all sleep [die a natural death], but we will all be changed—in a flash, in the twinkling of an eye…" (NIV)

We have to allow ourselves to die to an old lifestyle with old habits and beliefs in order to experience being born again.

I have realized that throughout scripture, "the dead" is among the living and not in reference to those who have gone by the way of the grave. Those who have died a physical death are referred to as "those who went by the grave."

The dead in Christ are those who like myself were nothing more than a "Pew Potato." I was in church physically, but mentally I was somewhere else, doing something else. I was spiritually dead. If this describes you, let me say that you just stepped closer to experiencing change than you realized. If you recognize this in your own life, you just took the first step. Congratulations! Let the process begin. There is no comparison between the death sentence and the gift of life.

The choice is still yours, but the question is, "What will you choose?"

Chapter Eleven

THE GIFT OF LIFE

"The person who believes God is set right by God—and that's the real life" (Galatians 3:12, MSG)

Not knowing who you are in Christ will hinder you from the ability to receive the gift of life. This is why it is vitally important to have knowledge of the Word of God. Knowledge of God's Word increases your faith and the ability to believe. Ignorance will only keep you struggling through life instead of living and enjoying it. God did not create you to struggle through life. He created you to reign in life. When we obtain knowledge of the Word of God, we come to understand who we are and what rightfully belongs to us. Understanding God's Word also gives to us power and dominion. Authority is given to us to rule over every circumstance and situation that rises up against us. We are also given creativity. We are to be creative in thought and action.

Galatians 6:5

"Each of you must take responsibility for doing the creative best you can with your own life." (MSG)

We all need to understand that as a born again Christian, we are responsible for our own actions and decisions. I have concluded that this is the reason why many do not want to be free, as with freedom comes responsibility. When a person exercises

When a person exercises their freedom to do or not to do, it is then their responsibility to accept the repercussions of their decision.

their freedom to do or not to do, it is then their responsibility to accept the repercussions of their decision. I have not always done so. When the repercussion came, I started the blame game. Once I began accepting the responsibility of my actions and decisions, I quickly began to see how I failed in other areas of my life as well— such areas as fatherhood, brotherhood, being a son, and being a husband.

I will never forget the day when reality checked me hard. I had been very negligent to my children and my wife due to the excessive drug use that had totally consumed me. I was at an emotional breaking point when I told my father that all I ever wanted to be was to be like my Paw-Paw. His reply was harsh, but true. "You are everything your Paw-Paw could not stand in a man," was his reply. In my old nature, that was totally absorbed with "self." I always sought to justify myself for what I was doing. Trust me when I say that self-absorption is a recipe for destruction. Instead of ruling over my circumstances and situations, they ruled over me. In the drug and alcohol world, there is an often-quoted phrase that says, "You have to do the drug and not let the drug do you." How stupid is this? This is as oxymoron as it gets! Why would anyone purchase a mind-altering drug and think they are going to do the drug? The drug is designed to change your thoughts, and that it did.

Religion is no different, as the effect it has had in our lives has changed our thinking from understanding our true identity to believing a lie. It has blinded us from the truth of who we are. It creates a false identity in you and will always tear you down. It causes you to become self-centered and survival-oriented. Now that I am in the process of my change, I have also realized that there is a process of overcoming the negative circumstances and situations that once controlled my life. They, too, were but hindrances to my creativity.

Why would anyone purchase a mind-altering drug and think they are going to do the drug? The drug is designed to change your thoughts and that it did.

My desperate desire for repentance challenged me to once again become creative with the talent of imagination. I have been born with a God-given talent in art and have become an accomplished artist in my own right. I have not exercised my artistic abilities in about twenty years other than using them in various construction trades, including carpentry skills. Now for the first time in my life, I write this book. As of now, it's my glory. I have no education as most may think. I barely graduated high school by the "skin of my teeth!" Literally!

Creativity is the exercising of the imagination, and trust me, I have one (smiling). I have always dreamed of the day that I would be free from the chains of addiction to drugs and alcohol. Over time, my dreams began to fade as the drugs reduced my ability to dream, or to imagine. My heart hurts and becomes heavy for those who are as I once was. I tell them to dream again! Dream again! Not to get into a detailed description of the biblical story of Joseph in Genesis chapter 37, I do want to say that when others step on your dreams, I suggest that you dream again! Dream again! This time, don't run and tell those who cannot understand you. Sometimes it's best to keep your dream between you and God until the dream comes true. Oh, I want to preach!

Creativity, the art of exercising the imagination, causes the invisible things of the spirit to be revealed in the visible realm of where we are. It brings heaven to earth! Creativity causes change—change of thoughts, emotions, and impulses that have been loosely fitted in our lives. We owe nothing, absolutely nothing to our past. Not one red cent!

I have always dreamed of the day that I would be free from the chains of addiction to drugs and alcohol.

Romans 8:12-13

"So don't you see that we don't owe this old do-it-yourself life one red cent. There's nothing in it for us, nothing at all. The best thing to do is give it a decent burial and get on with your new life." (MSG)

Verse 14 goes on to say that there are things to do and places to go! There are many places I long to see, and there are many things I long to do—such places as the Grand Canyon and Niagara Falls, and all places in between. I want to explore the United States, even the world as I do what I have always dreamed of doing—preaching the gospel of redemption. I want to shake the hands of those who have blazed the trail before me and say, "Thank you for the message of grace." I want to turn behind me and pull someone out of the hell that I once lived in into the wonderful new life in Christ Jesus that we have now come to know as "Graceland." I want to be a daddy to my girls. I want to be "Paw-Paw" to my grandbabies. I want to watch sunrises and sunsets from a porch swing; I want to do so with someone who can love me and my girls, and all my grandchildren, in the same way that I love and accept theirs. This is my dream-again dream.

Romans 8:15-17

"This resurrection life you received from God [the Gift of Life] is not a timid, grave-tending life. It is adventurously expectant, greeting God with a childlike 'What's next Papa?'

God's Spirit touches our spirits and confirms who we really are. We know who he is, and we know who we are: Father and children. And we know what we are going to get is what is coming to us—an unbelievable inheritance!" (MSG)

In this new life, we become children to the best Dad anyone could ever imagine. As creative as we are with imagination, I still can't fathom how much He really loves me. Whoever thought it to be too late for an awesome childhood! (smiling)

I want to turn behind me and pull someone out of the hell that I once lived in into the wonderful life in Christ Jesus that we have now come to know as "Graceland."

As I now have begun to live in this extravagant life of pure grace, it reminds me of my childhood years when I lived care free, enjoying being alive and exploring life as if there were no tomorrow. It's who I was then; it's who I am now, and I am loved by Him who created me to be me. I am overtaken by the thought of just how much He loves me. Now, all of a sudden, the word of two songs began to sing inside of me—"Good, Good Father" by Chris Tomlin and "How He Loves" by Kim Walker Smith.

The most quoted verse of the Bible has been without question John 3:16.

"For God so loved the world that He gave His only begotten son, that whosoever believeth in Him should not perish, but have everlasting life." (KJV)

Here again, we see the word "believe." Believing is the only requirement of the New Covenant. If we were to back up to the beginning of chapter 3 of the Book of John, we read of Jesus teaching Nicodemus concerning being born again. Remember what we discussed in chapter 10 of the importance of understanding the principle of being born again was so that we can receive the gift of life. Nicodemus was a member of the Jewish Council that sought to crucify Christ. However, there was something that intrigued his thoughts concerning the teachings of Jesus. Nicodemus reminds me of some people of today that I feel are honest seekers but quickly roll with the flow when others are present among them.

Jesus did not fit the mold of the Scribes and Pharisees that Nicodemus was associated with. Nicodemus' honesty was revealed in the fact that He contemplated the thought that he himself just might be wrong. If this were not the case, then he never would have sought Jesus' counsel privately. He began by asking, "How can a man be born when he is old?" (John 3:4, KJV).

Many today teach wrongly because they themselves were taught wrongly. I have finally come to a point to forgive those who mistaught the Word of God for the fact that they were doing the best they could with what they themselves had received. Nicodemus was willing to re-examine his believe system, and with an open mind, he sought the counsel of Jesus concerning the subject at hand. He was ready to lay down everything that religion had produced in search of truth. Nicodemus had spent a lifetime in a performance-based religious system that only produced empty ceremonies and unfulfilled obligations.

Religion is blinding and keeps you unable to see the truth of who you are. Religion is no different from the drugs and alcohol that once seemed to be the right thing to do, and was nothing more than a cover-up. They are both deceptive and manipulative of truth. And we wonder why people such as myself who has or is in the bondage of addiction to drugs and/or alcohol don't turn to most churches for help. There is no one that I have known on the streets that care to trade one bondage for another. It's like kissing your sister—ain't no future in it!

Upon closer examination of the story of Nicodemus, we see where he searched for understanding. I suggest that he received such understanding when his eyes were opened from the blinding religious system that he himself was a scholar of. I also suggest that this took place when he saw for himself the Son of God who hung suspended on an old rugged cross on Calvary's Hill. It is where the eyes of his understanding were opened, and he saw who he was for the first time—a child of God in the person of Jesus. The question of "how can a man be born again when he is old" was answered. Although Nicodemus was not mentioned again after his private meeting with Jesus until Jesus' death, I believe that he stayed by his side. Scripture does not speak of where Nicodemus was after his private meeting, but it does say that he brought myrrh and aloe to prepare Jesus' body for proper burial (John 19:38-42).

When we look upon the cross of Calvary we also see for ourselves the powerful work of redemption. In doing so, we see where our old nature died; we were baptized unto death, and were born again into newness of life through His resurrection.

The latter part of Romans 6:3 puts it like this:

"...we entered into the new country of grace—a new life in a new land." (MSG)

Looking also at Romans 6:2-4

"...we are those who have died to sin; how can we live in it any longer? Or don't you know that all of us who were baptized into Christ Jesus were baptized into His death? We were therefore buried with him through baptism into death in order that, just as Christ was raised from the dead through the glory of the Father, we too may live a new life." (NIV)

There are three major attributes found in the new covenant life.

- Acceptance
- Security
- Significance

As I now come to the end of my second phase of the discipleship program here at the Center of Hope, I have compared this second phase to the "Holy Place" or "Inner Court" of the Tabernacle of Moses (see chapter 26 of the Book of Exodus). The Holy Place represents a progression from our initial experience of repentance to a more intimate relationship with God. The Tabernacle was a tent that was set up in the desert during the time that the children of Israel had just exited out of the bondage of slavery in Egypt. God instructed Moses to assemble this tent so that there would be a dwelling place for Him among His people (Exodus 25:8).

In the new covenant life, we are the dwelling place of God. We are His Temple. God no longer dwells in a building built by man's hands but in His creation—you and me. We are the City of God, the New Jerusalem. God has moved out of a building into a person—that person being Jesus Christ, and as we become identified in Christ, we then become the dwelling place of God.

First Corinthians 3:16

"Don't you know that you yourselves are God's temple and that God's Spirit dwells in your midst?" (NIV)

The inner court of Moses Tabernacle is what I refer to as the room of identification. It is where we come to understand who we are. This is also what our phase II class does. It reveals who you are in Christ. It gives you an understanding of the work of redemption that was completed in Christ Jesus. The three attributes of acceptance, security and significance are the focuses of Phase II. In order for us to complete our Phase II course of study, we have to recite from memory what is considered The Faith Confessions. They are as follows:

- Acceptance

    - "I am God's child" (John 1:1)

    - "I am Christ's friend" (John 15:15)

    - "I am united with the Lord, and one Spirit with Him" (I Corinthians 6:17)

    - "I am a saint" (Ephesians 1:1)

    - "I have been adopted as God's child" (Ephesians 1:5)

    - "I have direct access to God through the Holy Spirit" (Ephesians 2:18)

God no longer dwells in a building built by man's hands but in His creation—you and I.

I want to pause here momentarily to say that the entire Book of Ephesians was written by the Apostle Paul and describes for us God's reason for redemption and how redemption is an ongoing perpetual daily changing process. As we come into more information of who we are, the process of our change begins to clear out the clutter of our past mistakes and failures, making space for grace. When we come to accept who we are based on the Word of God, and not on the basis of what we do or have done, we realize that we are not just striving to reach a destination, but rather we are finding a resting place in Jesus. We find our rest in the finished work of redemption. We no longer seek a destination, but we begin to flow from a position of rest. It is who we are based on His work in us and not on our works seeking to obtain a position. Who we had become based on what we did is not our true identity.

Ephesians 2:8

"For it is by grace you have been saved, through faith—and this is not from yourselves, it is the gift of God." (NIV)

- Security

    o "I am free from condemnation" (Romans 8:1-2)

    o "I cannot be separated from the love of God" (Romans 8:35-39)

Romans 8:35-39 speaks the most to me personally—this passage of Scripture tells me that there is absolutely nothing that I have ever done that will cause Him to close the door to His heart. Nothing means nothing! It also tells me that there is nothing that I can do right to cause Him to love me anymore than he already does. The only thing that can and does change is me.

    o "I am confident that the good work that God has begun in me will be completed" (Philippians 1:6)

    o "I am a citizen of heaven" (Philippians 3:20)

    o "I have not been given a spirit of fear, but of power, love and a sound mind" (I Timothy 1:7)

II Timothy 1:7 also tells me that in this new life, God does not want me to be afraid or shy in this gift of life that He has given me. You also do not have to be scared of what is in store for you as you venture into this new spacious life that I have come to know as grace. We need not be afraid to explore this new adventurous life-filled life, as it is this new life itself that empowers you to do whatever it is that needs to be done. It is the gift of grace because it is free unto those who choose to believe.

    o "I am born of God and the evil one cannot touch me" (I John 5:18)

- Significance

  - "I am a personal witness of Christ" (Acts 1:8)

  - "I am God's Temple" (I Corinthians 3:16)

  (We have previously discussed the fact that we are the true temple of God.)

  - "I am God's co-worker" (II Corinthians 6:1)

  - "I'm seated with Christ in the heavenly realm" (Ephesians 2:4)

  - "I may approach God with freedom and confidence" (Ephesians 3:12)

  - "I can do all things through Christ who strengthens me" (Philippians 4:13)

All of these faith confessions tell us who we are in Christ and what rightfully belongs to us as children of God. All these blessings are available to us today. Hebrews 4:7 tells us that God Himself had set a certain day, and that day was called "today." As I begin to bring this chapter to a close, I want to say that there is not a final destination point in change. Change is a lifelong process, and we need to always remain open-minded enough to not fall into the deception of thinking "we got this."

Change is a lifelong process, and we need to always remain open-minded enough to not fall into deception of thinking "we got this."

Although a process is defined as a series of actions that are taken in order to reach a particular end, the only end that we should seek is the end of an old lifestyle. My old lifestyle of drug and alcohol use and abuse had to come to an end. Philippians 3:12-14 tells us that we do not come to a finish line; we come to the person of Jesus Christ who He Himself is our finish line.

The Center of Hope here in Anniston, Alabama has given me something to take hold of. That something is Jesus and an understanding of the work of redemption that He Himself completed in my stead. They helped me to see myself for who I really am, a child of God! In doing so, it has enabled me to let go of the "me" that I was. In my old self, I knew no other way out than death. Death really is the answer, but it's just not a physical death that needs to take place. The death of Jesus is what saves us from having to die a death unto ourselves.

John 3:15 tells us that anyone who believes in Jesus Christ and the work of redemption that was completed in His death, burial, and resurrection will receive the "gift of life." We do not have to live up to anyone's standards, nor do we have to live above what we know.

Although a process is defined as a series of actions that are taken in order to reach a particular end, the only end that we should seek is the end of an old lifestyle.

Philippians 3:15-16

"All of us, then, who are mature should take such a view of things [come to understand]. And if on some point you think differently, that too God will make clear to you. Only let us live up to what we have already attained." (NIV)

In the remaining verses of chapter 3 in Philippians, it instructs us to join others that have come into an understanding of the gospel of Jesus Christ. The gospel is the good news of Jesus who is our pattern to live by in the newness of life. It also states that there are those who live as enemies of the cross, and that their destination is destruction. However, our citizenship is in the heavenlies.

Let me close with Philippians 3:21.

"Who by the power that enables him to bring everything under his control, will transform our lowly bodies so that we will be like His glorious body." (NIV)

We are who He is—the glory of God!

I pray that I have laid a foundation on which you can build on as you yourself search for a change.

The choice is yours.

Receive it today—the "Gift of Life."

"

Philippians 3:15-16:

"All of us who are mature should take a view of things, and if on some point you think differently, that too God will make clear to you. Only let us live up to what we have already attained." (NIV)

Chapter Twelve

DON'T BE AFRAID!

Fear is a hindrance and will keep you more bound than free. It will keep you from receiving all that God has for you in your new life.

II Timothy 1:7

"For God has not given us the spirit of fear; but of power, and of love, and of a sound mind." (KJV)

Reading through First and Second Timothy, I began to see how Timothy and I had several similarities—such similarities as fear and low self-worth. I have come to realize that most preachers do, also. I guess this qualifies me to preach! (smiling)

In order for us to experience real love, we have to learn to trust God's Word. We will never trust what we know nothing about. This is why we need to read the Word (our Bibles) so that we can obtain knowledge of Him and what He has already provided for us in our new life, while waiting for our arrival. Knowledge of the Word of God will open the eyes of our understanding allowing us to see the things that are readily available to us.

Romans 5:20 (NIV) tells us that there is an unlimited supply of God's love for us.

"...but where sin increased, grace increased all the more."

Fear is not of God. Fear comes only from the devil when he speaks accusations to our wounded souls. Such accusations as— "How can you trust God after what He has allowed to happen to you?" "Do you really think you can preach and people listen to you after all the stuff you have done?" The old saying, "Sticks and stones may break my bones, but words will never hurt me," is a lie! It is as much of a lie as the accusations that the devil shouts at you in an attempt to keep you from being who God created you to be. Words are powerful and are used to build you up or tear you down.

The first words spoken in the beginning were creative in power as God Himself spoke creation into existence. Satan was also creative in his speech to Adam and Eve in the Garden of Eden, as found in Genesis, chapter three. His motive was to destroy the man that God had created. This is why it is so vitally important to know who you listen to.

Upon loss of our esteem and worth, we give place to shame, and our shame will cause us to fall back into our old life pattern of "covering up."

We have all been guilty of allowing what someone says to us tear us down. When we allow Satan to speak to us, we give him permission to tear us down. In these tearing down moments, we lose our self-esteem and our self-worth. Upon loss of our esteem and worth, we give place to shame, and our shame will cause us to fall back into our old life pattern of covering up. This is exactly what took place with Adam and Eve in the Garden when they "got scared." Let's look and see for ourselves.

Genesis 3:8-10

"Then the man and his wife heard the sound of the Lord God as he was walking in the garden in the cool of the day, and they hid from the Lord God among the trees of the garden. But the Lord God called to the man, 'Where are you?' He answered, 'I heard you in the garden, and I was afraid because I was naked; so I hid.'" (NIV)

I was no different as I also began listening to the wrong voice and began seeking gratification through the self-effort attempts to become something I already was. Sound stupid? It is! This is what we do when we don't know who we are. As I look back, I see where I had no power to resist the temptations of this world because I had no knowledge of the Word of God. I knew only enough to be dangerous with it.

I know who I am based on who God says I am.

I do not view Adam and Eve as rebels without a cause. I just see them as gullible. They, like myself, simply believed a lie. They were no more rebellious than I was; yet, we were both foolish in the choices that we made when we exercised our freedom to choose. It was when I exercised my freedom of choice, and I chose to do the wrong thing, that I placed myself into the bondage of my wrong. I have concluded that freedom is most useful when we choose to do what is right.

I am no longer controlled by the fear of making bad decisions, nor do I fear the thoughts that seem to find their way back into my head that attempt to tell me that I have wasted my life and will never amount to anything. I recognized the voices in my head as lies, and I do not entertain them with my attention. I just smile and say, "These thoughts do not belong to me anymore as they are not mine to own." I am now able to do so because of the knowledge I have obtained by reading God's Word. I know who I am based on who God says I am. I now know what the Word of God says about me. This is how we tear down the strongholds of thoughts, ideas, and suggestions that attempt to exalt themselves over the Word that God Himself has spoken over us.

Romans 12:2 gives reason for us to read and study God's Word concerning us:

"Do not conform to the pattern of this world, but be transformed by the renewing of your mind. Then you will be able to test and approve what God's will is—his good, pleasing and perfect will." (NIV)

If we do not read and study God's Word to prove what God's will is for our lives, we will remain in the depths of our guilt and shame. We will continue to give way to the resentments of past mistakes and failures creating within itself a fear of the future. Fear of the future will cause you to only see yourself the way you were. If you remain focused on the way you were, you will eventually return to where you have been.

I am no longer controlled by the fear of making bad decisions, nor do I fear the thoughts that seem to find their way back into my head that attempt to tell me that I have wasted my life and will never amount to anything.

There is no fear in the Kingdom of God. There is only righteousness, peace, and joy.

Romans 14:17

"For the Kingdom of God is not a matter of eating and drinking, but of righteousness, peace and joy in the Holy Spirit." (NIV)

The Kingdom of God is where you live. It is where He rules and reigns, and the earth is where we are. It is here upon this earth that we are to be the expressed image of God. We are to be the expression of righteousness. Righteousness is what empowers us to make right choices and decisions.

II Corinthians 5:20(b)-21:

"...we implore you on Christ's behalf: Be reconciled to God. God made him who had no sin to be sin for us, so that in him we might become the righteousness of God." (NIV)

Fear of the future will cause you to only see yourself the way you were.

Righteousness is what causes us to operate in the spirit of obedience. Our righteousness was the result of Christ's obedience to God the Father.

Romans 5:19

"For just as through the disobedience of the one man the many were made sinners, so also through the obedience of the one man the many will be made righteous." (NIV)

We are to be the expression of peace. Jesus Himself is our peace. When we accept Jesus into our hearts, He replaces our fears, strengthens our faith, and reveals to us of who we are.

Philippians 4:7

"And the peace of God which transcends all understanding, will guard your hearts and your minds in Christ Jesus."(NIV)

When we accept Jesus into our hearts, He replaces our fears, strengthens our faith, and reveals to us of who we are.

It is Jesus Himself who becomes our very life. When we have Jesus in our hearts, we are no longer controlled by fear.

We are also to be the expression of joy. Joy is your strength, your spiritual muscle. Nehemiah 8:10 states that the joy of the Lord is our strength. Nehemiah commands us to celebrate with great joy! (Neh. 8:12). Joy is also what brings you rest. It comes from knowing and understanding the work of redemption as finished and complete. True strength is best expressed when we learn how to let go of the things that keep us in bondage—such things as drugs and alcohol—as well as religion. There were many things that I had to let go of, but drugs and alcohol were my crutches.

As I stated earlier in this book, it was in the summer of 1979 when the tragic automobile accident occurred that claimed the lives of my grandparents, my aunt, and infant cousin. That left another cousin and myself as the survivors. It also left me with third degree burns, lacerations, extreme road rash, and a double compound fracture to my left leg. I was placed in a full cast for a little over six months. I had to learn how to walk on crutches for the first couple of months, and that I did! I could fly in the wind on those ole crutches without ever placing a foot on the ground. I would pick both feet up and walk through mud holes without getting my feet wet. I could even go up and down the high school stairs as if I was an escalator.

If you remain focused on the way you were, you will eventually return to where you have been.

However, the real challenge came when it was time to put the crutches away and begin to walk on my own. It was much like the beginning of my change when I put away my crutches of drugs and alcohol and began to learn how to walk without the support of my friends. My friends that I leaned on to get me through each day had now left me standing alone to face the fear of falling, and falling is what I did. I would fall walking across flat ground, and my first attempt at the staircase sent me tumbling down the steps like a basketball. It also got me another trip to the doctor for repairs. Recovery has been the same as I have fallen and fallen again and again and have been in and out of rehabs trying to put all the broken pieces back together again.

Fear always kept me from ever experiencing a permanent change—just as I was fearful of never walking again as I once did. Fact is that I did walk again, and my leg was stronger than ever! It is not until we let go and take that first step will we ever know what our future holds.

Letting go is the hard part. For me, it took everything in me to come to the decision to let go and trust that God will do what He says He will do. It is hard to let go of things that you think you need to survive. As hard and as exhaustive as it is, I have come to know that it's not as exhaustive as holding on. Once I let go, the feeling of free falling left me breathless; and within seconds, I fell into the safety of His arms. As He lifted me to my feet, I turned around to see from whence I had fallen, and I really wasn't that far (smiling). Letting go wasn't as hard as I made it out to be. I knew I had to let go of the drugs and alcohol or die. I had no desire to live, but I didn't want to really die, either.

I knew I had to let go of the drugs and alcohol or die. I had no desire to live, but I didn't want to die, either.

What I wanted was rest—rest for my weary soul, and rest for the fatigue of my mind. Rest seemed impossible and sleep was out of the question. Our motto was, "We will get all the rest we need when we die." I didn't realize then just how much truth is spoken in this phrase. We really do find rest in our death, just not a physical death. I did seek rest for my physical body, but when I would take time to do so, I would be overtaken with guilt for not doing anything. So, I would get up and go again. My body was worn out, and my mind became my enemy. I was weary and worn out, and I began to feel old and ugly. I knew I needed a physical rest as I only averaged around two hours of sleep per night for a period of around ten months, and this was after I had just pulled a twenty-eight day stretch of little to no sleep. God never intended for us to live an exhaustive lifestyle.

Matthew 11:28-29

"Come to me, all you who are weary and burdened, and I will give you rest. Take my yoke upon you and learn from me, for I am gentle and humble in heart, and you will find rest for your souls." (NIV)

There is a song entitled, "Come All You Weary" by the artist "Thrice" that I have come to love and appreciate because the words speak to my heart in a way that I feel that it is God Himself that speaks to me.

Letting go is the hard part. For me, it took everything in me to come to the decision to let go and trust that God will do what He says He will do.

Rest is a gift, and that gift is the person of Jesus Christ. When we refuse Him, we welcome the weight of this world upon our shoulders. When we come to Jesus, we find such rest. When our souls are rested, we will experience an unspeakable joy that God Himself completes in us.

Romans 14:17

"It's what God does with your life as He sets it right, puts it together, and completes it with joy." (MSG)

God knew the importance of rest, as He Himself rested from all of His work of creating the heavens and the earth:

Genesis 2:2-3 (NIV)

"By the seventh day God had finished the work that He had been doing; so on the seventh day, he rested from all His work. Then God blessed the seventh day and made it holy, because on it he rested from all the work of creating that He had done."

The word *rested* found here in both verses are descriptive of the words *stop* or *cease.* I would like to suggest that on the seventh day, God ceased from His labors of creating so that He could take time and come to earth to enjoy a conversation with His creation man.

I have not totally accepted that God has completely stopped creating for the simple fact that I have yet to come into the complete fullness of who I am. I really do believe there is more to come. I have not found any evidence in Scripture that would suggest that God is finished. However, I do suggest that when the work of redemption was completed, Jesus spoke saying, "It is finished," and God responded, "I am satisfied." Nowhere does it imply that God or Jesus is finished. What was finished was the work of redemption that God did in Christ for and as us.

Genesis 2:1 says that what was finished was the creating of the heavens and the earth. Then as Jesus hung suspended in the air on Calvary's Hill, the work of redemption was completed and finished. For this reason is why I have personally concluded that God "ain't finished with me yet!" (smiling). Ain't may not be proper English, but it sho' is good Southern talk.

When we learn how to cease from our labors, we will begin finding comfort from the posture of rest. I also would suggest that it was in a posture of rest that God came into the realm of this earth to enjoy fellowship with His greatest creation—man. Scripture described it as "in the cool of the day." I have always enjoyed a nice ride in the country back roads just before night fall. It is the coolest part of the day, and in the setting of the evening sun, I find the most beautiful and vibrant colors in the sky. There is but a small window of time before the darkness comes, but the time it takes to prepare for that moment is worth it.

It was in this moment of each day that God would take His evening walk through His garden, His paradise, to enjoy conversation with Adam and his wife. He seeks to do the same with you and me. He longs for us to realize that our relationship with Him has been restored. As I have mentioned earlier in this chapter, words have creative power and how listening to the wrong words from the wrong person (including some preachers) can tear you down. This is precisely what happened with Adam and Eve as they stood before the Tree of Knowledge and listened to the serpent as he manipulated the Word of God for his own purpose. They listened to this wrong voice and believed a lie that resulted in a broken relationship with God.

When God spoke saying, "Where are you?" Adam's reply was, "I was hiding because I was naked." The immediate response of God was, "Who told you that you were naked?" In other words, God was saying, "Who have you been listening to?" So, the next time you feel you are naked and ashamed (exposed of your wrongs), and you experience the feelings of regret and disqualification for the righteousness, peace, and joy that rightfully belong to you, tell the voice that is speaking to you, "Shut that mouth!" "Shut that mouth" is a statement that is made here at the Center of Hope when there is negative talk among the students. Trust me, whenever negativity starts, "Shut that mouth" resounds from around every corner, down every hallway, and even from the showers and dorm rooms.

I have finally come to experience true joy in my life in a way that I never thought possible. I find this joy in the moments that I am able to assist other students here at the Center to come to an understanding of who they are. When I can say or do something that helps them to step closer to their purpose in life, I am fulfilling my purpose as well. In doing so, I become overtaken with an inexpressible joy. My joy comes when I place others before myself. Remembering something that Sims used to tell me about joy was that joy comes when you learn how to put Jesus first in your life, others second, and then yourself (JOY).

It's always a joy to receive gifts from others, but there is an unspeakable joy that comes when you give the gifts of righteousness, peace, and joy that have been given you unto others. If you do not have them, it is only because you have not received them. They are yours for the taking! Don't be scared and come on and get you some!

The choice is yours. (I got mine).

I have finally come to experience true joy in my life in a way that I never thought possible.

Chapter Thirteen

THIS IS LOVE

In the first part of chapter 12, I had stated that when we listen to the lies of the devil, we give him permission to tear us down and rob our self-esteem and self-worth. However, when we come to realize that we are loved by God, we begin to regain our self-esteem and self-worth. Our fears begin to vanish as the truth of God's Word begins to permeate our hearts. This does not happen because we first loved God, but because He first loved us and gave Himself to us so that we can come into a complete understanding of who we are (maturity). I feel the preacher sneaking up on me again! (smile).

I John 4:9-10

"This is how God showed His love for us: God sent His only begotten Son into the world so we might live through Him. This is the kind of love we are talking about, not that we once upon a time loved God; but that He loved us and sent His only son as a sacrifice to clear away our sins and the damage they've done to our relationship with God." (MSG)

There are so many scriptures that list the attributes of God's love for us that it leaves me with my jaw dropped open and my eyes bulged out like a frog in a hail storm. When I asked God where to start, He simply said, "Share your heart." So here I go.

I am quickly reminded of scripture found in the book of John where Jesus reinstated Peter after he had returned to doing what he had done before Jesus had called him into his discipleship, and that was fishing. Peter and several other disciples had been out fishing when Jesus appeared on the shore with breakfast cooking on an open fire. Jesus invited them once again to come eat with Him. After they ate, Jesus asked Peter, "Do you truly love me more than these?" Peter replied, "You know that I love you." Jesus said, "Feed my lambs."

We have all read the story, but for those who haven't, it is found in John chapter 21. Jesus had asked Peter if he loved Him three times. I personally feel that this possibly represented three types of love—*storge, philia*, and *agape. Storge* is the type of love that a parent would have toward a child. Jesus did command Peter to first feed His lambs. *Philia* is a type of love that is brotherly. It is expressed when we take care of each other. Jesus commanded Peter the second time to "take care of my sheep." Then there is *agape.* It is the love of God Himself and the kind in which we are commanded to be the expression to all (including our enemies).

I feel as I have always loved God, but up until now, I would have to honestly say that my love for God has been conditional. "If you do this, then I will do that" was often my conditions when I would feel God prompting me to come to Him. I often would answer in question, "Why? What have You done for me lately?" It's funny how we easily forget all that He really has done for us when we don't get what we want, when we want it. It reminds me of the children of Israel as they wandered around the wilderness complaining that God hasn't done anything for them but led them out into a desert to die. They failed to realize that He was ever present and ever providing. Then on top of it all, their youth was preserved.

I know who I am based on who God says I am.

When we ask what God has done for us, we often pull out our single-shot shotgun loaded with John 3:16 and quote:

> "For God so loved the world that He gave His only begotten son, that whosoever believeth in Him shall not perish, but have everlasting life." (KJV)

This gives us an understanding of *why,* but more importantly to me was *when* He did so. We know that corporately speaking it was on Calvary's Cross more than two thousand years ago, but subjectively speaking, it was on August of 2016 when God showed His love toward me in a tangible way. And guess what? I wasn't in a church, nor was I on bended knees at an altar with all the elders of the Church surrounding me. No, I was sitting at my kitchen table with a needle in my arm. As I began to inject a lethal dose of methamphetamine, I began crying out loud for God to forgive me for what I was attempting to do as I had all intentions of taking my life that evening. But God!

God showed His love for me as He began to reveal to me of Jesus hanging suspended on the cross. I could feel the pain and agony that Jesus Himself was experiencing, and all of a sudden my pain and agony felt minute.

All the hell and all the pain that I have ever experienced could not compare to the smallest morsel that I tasted that night. It was just hours before that I had called my parents in Georgia to let them know that I was turning my phone off and that they would not be able to contact me. They pleaded with me to allow them to come get me and take me to receive help. The last thing I remember saying was that if they did not hear from me in the next several days then they could call 911.

Over the course of about seven days (not sure to be exact), it was God and I. My point to be made is that God showed me His love in the death, burial, and resurrection of His begotten son, Jesus. He showed His unconditional love toward me at the very lowest point in my life. It was in a moment that I was attempting to take my own life that He gave me His. It was in that very moment that my fears began departing from me, and my healing process began. The fears of failure, acceptance, and rejection were at the top of the list. Fear of rejection of others sat second only to my fear of a "someday judgment from God." Little did I realize then that my day of judgment was actually behind me, but the revelation of it became a reality to me over the following several days. It was the revelation of Jesus Christ and the complete work of redemption that set me free. It was the gift of love.

I have often read through the Book of First John, but never from the Message/Remix. When I did, it told the story of my experience.

> I John 4:16-18
>
> "God is love, when we take up permanent residence in a life of love, we live in God and God lives in us. This way, love has the run of the house, becomes at home and mature in us, so that we're free from worry on judgement day. Our standing in the world is identical with Christ's. There is no room in love for fear. Well-formed love banishes fear. Since fear is crippling, a fearful life—fear of death, fear of judgment—is one not yet fully formed in love." (MSG)

There is a powerful truth that God showed me concerning judgement. That truth is that judgment is not always punishable. A judgment of *not guilty* is not a punishment. It is what I call the Gospel. Gospel defined is *good news,* and the verdict of not guilty is good news to anyone.

One of the elderly women died in my arms as she was begging me to not let her die.

One of the most difficult situations (if not the most difficult) that I have ever dealt with was a time that I was charged with vehicular manslaughter in the first degree by DUI. It was a Saturday afternoon, and I was on my way home from work. I was only a few miles from home when two elderly women pulled out in front of me, and I broad-sided their vehicle. My estimated speed upon impact was fifty miles per hour. I don't care to go into full detail, but to make a long story short, one of the elderly women died in my arms as she was begging me to not let her die. I had only blown a .06 on the alcohol breath test (the intoxication level in Georgia is .08). However, when a fatality is involved, they can charge you as low as .04. I was facing a ten-year sentence, and after approximately 18 months of court sessions, it was now "judgment day." When judgment was passed that day, and the judge ruled "not guilty," that was absolutely good news to me.

> *Gospel defined is "good news," and the verdict of not guilty is good news to anyone.*

I see many Christians today that live their entire Christian life in fear of what most seem to think is a someday great white throne judgment a lot like the way I lived in those 18 months prior to my judgment—in fear! I have also witnessed them make the same mistake I had also made just shortly after my freedom came. Though I was free, I still felt guilty and placed myself back under the judgment trap of self. When it came to judging myself, I was ruthless! The verdict of "not guilty" brought only a temporary freedom because my freedom was invaded by the sense of guilt and shame as the memory of an innocent elderly woman's last words to me were, "Please don't let me die!"

Most Christians, like myself, have found freedom but have sabotaged their freedom for the simple fact that they don't know how to act or live in such freedom. For this reason, we allow fear of the unknown to take us back into our comfort zone of bondage. We become spiritually institutionalized. We need to open ourselves up to the love of God and learn how to accept His mercy and grace. If you feel undeserving, then let me remind you that grace is undeserved favor, and mercy is not for the innocent.

Love is what sets us free. It's what changes us from just surviving into actually living. Truly living in God's reality and not our imaginations.

I John 3:18-20

"My dear children, let's not just talk about love; let's practice real love. This is the only way we'll know we're living truly, living in God's reality. It's also the way to shut down debilitating self-criticism, even when there is something to it (such as was in my situation). For God is greater than our worried hearts and knows more about us than we do ourselves." (MSG)

If you feel undeserving, then let me remind you that grace is undeserved favor, and mercy is not for the

---

Self-criticism truly is debilitating. Self-destruction is the work of self-righteousness, and worry is fear-based. We need to come to the realization that God is greater than our fears, and He seeks to take care of us in every situation. Verse 21 was the "icing on the cake" for me.

I John 3:21

"And friends, once that's taken care of and we're no longer accusing or condemning ourselves, we're bold and free before God!" (MSG)

So, love is really what sets us free. Now that we have established that love has set us free, we must also know the way of love. We need to learn how to walk in the ways of love, and I know no other book or chapter in the Bible that shows this way better than I Corinthians chapter 13.

I Corinthians 13:1 states:

"If I speak in the tongues (or languages) of men and of angels, but have not love, I am only a resounding gong of a clanging cymbal." (NIV)

The message refers to us as a "creaking of a rusty gate." Verse two and three tell us that we can do good things, but they avail us nothing if we do not do them in love. I say that "if it ain't from the heart, then don't even start."

People really do know if you do things from the heart, or if you're just seeking approval of others. There are those even here at the Center of Hope student body that know how to clang their cymbals seeking approval of other students. I have realized that the only ones that they impress are those who lack knowledge.

I love the way The Message/Remix defines love in verses four through seven.

- Love never gives up.
- Love cares more for others than for self.
- Love doesn't want what it doesn't have.
- Love doesn't strut.
- Doesn't have a swelled head.
- Doesn't force itself on others.
- Isn't always "me first."
- Doesn't fly off the handle.
- Doesn't keep score of the sins of others.
- Doesn't revel when others grovel.
- Takes pleasure in the flowering of truth.
- Puts up with anything.
- Trust God always.
- Always looks for the best.
- Never looks back, but keeps going to the end.

When we live the life of love as it is meant to be, we have reached maturity. It is when we put away our childish, argumentative ways and reactions. My wife, Kimberly, has been a true example of the way we all should live. She has never lost the "little girl" in her, yet she is a true woman. She giggles and smiles and finds satisfaction in the simple things in life. She loves to watch butterflies and birds. She talks to the frogs and sleeps to the sound of crickets playing an evening serenade. I have often told her that I hope she never loses touch with that little girl inside of her. First Corinthians 13:11 speaks of this "child-likeness," yet we all have misinterpreted it to say that we are not to be childlike. It does not say this. It does say that we are to put away our "childish" ways. For most, including myself, we have failed to recognize the difference between the two. Let's look at it from scripture.

I Corinthians 13:11

"When I was a child, I talked like a child, I thought like a child, I reasoned like a child. When I became a man, I put childish ways behind me." (NIV)

Notice here how Paul the Apostle stated that he talked, thought, and reasoned like a child, but when he became a man, he put away "childish" ways. Nowhere did he state that he gave up his "child-likeness." What he did do was put away his childish behavior. In other words, he changed his reactions to situations and his responses to others.

Jesus' own response to his disciples question, "Who is the greatest in the kingdom of heaven?" (Matthew chapter 18, verse 3). Jesus' response was, "I tell you the truth, unless you become like little children, you will never enter the kingdom of heaven." Jesus was not saying to become childish and start whining and crying because someone sat in your seat at church, but to come to Him humble in spirit and willing to receive the love of God without conditions as I once did.

A child is humble, teachable, and most of all, trusting. These "childlike" characteristics are what we are to ever hold onto. They are what qualifies us to become participants in the kingdom of heaven. For most of us, we have to become disconnected with these childlike virtues because we have misunderstood the message of the Apostle Paul. Once again, this is how our lives are affected when the Bible is improperly represented. So many of us feel as if we do not qualify for the life of love because of the brokenness of past mistakes and failures. I personally know that there has always been the presence of love in my life as it is evident in the fact that I still live to tell of it. I call it grace. Just as God so loved the world that He gave His only begotten son, so that we may have life, I now choose to show my love toward Him by turning toward His grace.

So many of us feel as if we do not qualify for the life of love because of the brokenness of past mistakes and failures.

I want to close this chapter with I Corinthians 14:1 (The Message /Remix):

"Go after a life of love as if your life depended on it—because it does. Give yourselves to the gifts God gives you. Most of all to proclaim His truth."

As you begin to discover the gift of love in your life, you will begin to discover the real you. If no one has told you lately that they love you, then let me say that Jesus and Ken love you (smiling).

I dedicate this chapter to my wife, Kimberly Dawn Meadors. Thank you for bringing love back into my life. I'm sorry for not knowing how to properly accept it. I now understand what you meant when you would tell me that I had to learn how to stop and smell the roses. I miss you in my life. (PS: Happy Valentine's Day).

> *As you begin to discover the gift of love in your life, you will begin to discover the real you.*

Chapter Fourteen

A FINISHED WORK WITH UNFINISHED BUSINESS

Matthew 28:18-20

"Jesus, undeterred, went right ahead and gave his charge. 'God authorized and commanded me to commission you; go out and train everyone you meet, far and near, in this way of life, marking them by baptism in the threefold name Father, Son, and Holy Spirit. Then instruct them in the practice of all I have commanded you. I will be with you as you do this, day after day, right up to the end of 'the age.'" (MSG)

It is for this reason God has preserved my life. For this reason I have survived life-threatening after life-threating events that are even more numerable than those I have mentioned in previous chapters. The reason I live is to "go tell" others of the miracle of life and of God's unlimited mercy and the aggressive forgiveness of grace.

The reason for this book is so that I can tell what God has done in me and for me and to let others know that He waits with an expectation of your return unto Him so He can be the same for you. As I have stated, I have known that I was called to preach my entire life. Yet, I have just recently fully accepted it—in the moment that I verbally told God to do with me as He has purposed. I also reminded Him that I was unqualified and undeserving of the honor. It was within a few short days God spoke a response to me through the prophetic voice of Pastor Gary Burns, our senior pastor here at the Center of Hope. It was a Sunday morning service, and as he was preaching, he paused momentarily and said, "Wow! I don't know who this is for, but God does not call the qualified, He qualifies who He calls." I just smiled and said, "Thank you God." We are all undeserving, but that's what qualifies us for grace.

Thinking over the ministry of Jesus Himself, I realized that the disciples whom He called to follow Him did not qualify to be preachers either, especially Peter. Peter was but a man's man by the standards of the world. He was a fisherman. I was raised running up and down the banks of the mighty Mississippi River and have known personally several commercial fishermen. They are often referred to as "river rats" because of the smell of the river that penetrates deep into their leather tough skin. Even after they shower, they still have the smell of the river on them. I say this in honor and not of shame as they are a tough breed of men. I have also lost several friends to the "river with no mercy." My grandfather nearly lost his life at an early age due to the swiftness of the river's water when he was knocked off of the river barge that he worked on as an engineer.

The reason I live is to "go tell" others of the miracle of life and of God's unlimited mercy and the aggressive forgiveness of grace.

When I read of Peter being a fisherman, I think of the men I knew. When Jesus bid Peter, "Come follow me, and I will make you a fisher of men," Peter accepted the call and got out of the boat and followed Jesus taking with him the stench of the boat still on him. This same Peter was the one who preached the first anointed sermon under the power of the Holy Spirit on the Day of Pentecost where three thousand people were added to the discipleship (Acts 2:14-21).

In chapter two of Acts, we read how the disciples were all together in one place, in one mind, and one accord. I suggest that the single focus or topic for discussion was that of the finished work of redemption. When we as Christians become single-focused on Calvary's cross, we will experience without warning a sound, a force that breaks through the barriers of self. And, like a wildfire, it will begin to purge, to burn up everything ungodly in our lives. It's called the indwelling of the Holy Spirit! (See Acts 2:1-4). It is when we realize that we are in our "last days." When the Holy Spirit moves into us and breathes the very life of God Himself, He burns up everything ungodly; and, the world, the life as we knew it is destroyed.

This is exactly what took place in the Upper Room. The Holy Spirit came in as a mighty rushing wind, and God moved into man. He made His abode in us. This indwelling of God's Holy Spirit was for the purpose of empowering and equipping us for ministry. It was for teaching us how to speak into the lives of others. Peter tells us how we do this in Acts 2:38-39.

First, you change your life, turn to God and be baptized so that your sins be forgiven (repent), and then receive the gift of life—the Holy Spirit. Peter continued to urge the people (as do I) to get out while you can from a sick and stupid culture—the sick and stupid culture of sin. I personally speak to those who are as I was, bound in the sick and stupid culture of drugs and alcohol, "Get out while you can!"

When the Holy Spirit moves into us and breathes the very life of God, He burns up everything ungodly; and, the world, the life as we knew it is destroyed.

My dad once told me that if I did not change my lifestyle that there would come a time or an age (as in years) in which it will become impossible to change outside of a miracle from God. I am that miracle, but oh, what I would have given to have listened to him then! Please listen and learn from the mistakes I have made. Listen to me now when I say that the hell that you go through trying to do it your way is a long hard road that leads to nowhere, and there is no guarantee that you will live to tell. There is a chance, a slight chance, as was with myself, but the chance is not worth the risk of dying.

It was also once said to me that a wise person learns from the mistakes of others. Please let my mistakes be your lessons learned and save yourself a lot of trouble, pain, and regret. Never think that the mistakes that you have already made disqualifies you for ministry. Ministry goes way beyond a pulpit and the four walls of a church. Ministry is simply helping others to come into a knowledge of who they are and to tap into their true God-given potentials. It's about reaching out into the unknown from your place of comfort and helping others who are in need. There are the homeless and hungry, the poor and needy that all carry the scars of a broken heart. Is the church that you attend experiencing increase? If not, then I suggest you re-evaluate your definition and motive of what you consider your outreach program.

> *Please let my mistakes be your lessons learned and save yourself a lot of trouble, pain, and regret.*

It has been approximately fifteen years ago that Sims and I, along with my dad, and Jim and Linda LeBlanc founded the recovery support group known as "Miracles in Action." It was birthed at Cedar Lake Christian Center in Cedartown, Georgia and accredited by the late Bishop David Huskins as the vehicle that brought an increase in church growth. This was accomplished by reaching into the streets and changing people's perspective of themselves—one heart at a time. Although Miracles in Action does not belong to any church organization or any other religious group, it has taken a hard lick from church members who have attempted to take control of it. Miracles in Action is its own ministry with only one purpose, and that is to share the love of Jesus to those who are in bondage of any form, including religion. Then we place them in

Christian-based discipleship programs such as the Center of Hope here in Anniston, Alabama who can guide them as they grow into maturity.

My heart's desire is to create a list of grace-filled churches from across the United States of America that will make themselves available to graduates of the Center of Hope that have no home church to return home to—a church that the graduates can go to as a follow-up as they go back out into the real world. I cannot over emphasize the need for more churches to get involved in outreach ministry.

There is a hillside here at the Center of Hope with a landscape of wooden crosses with the names of previous students who graduated or left the discipleship program too soon. None of them that I know of had a church body to follow up with them. The weight of the world was too much for a yearling Christian that received them back with open arms and an open grave. Some have been found in the back alleys of the streets that they once loved. Others have been found, just days and even hours after leaving, in a motel room dead from drug overdoses. There are others such as myself who have been fortunate enough to make it back into the safety of the program and live to tell. I guess favor really isn't fair sometimes. I count my blessings daily!

Every day that I awaken, I thank God for the gift of life. I thank Him for my health, wealth, and wisdom that He has blessed me with and the increase of them with each passing day. Though my sails have been torn, and my ship beaten by the winds and waves, the anchor holds. I often wonder how powerful of a minister those whose name is written on the wood crosses could have been if there was a church available in their community that was able to nourish the seed that was planted in them here at the center.

I often find myself telling others of a story that I once heard concerning the African lion. The story was told from a National Geographic documentation. In this documentation, the commentator stated that when a lion roars, all the animals in the animal kingdom respects him from a distance of around a one-mile radius. When a lion becomes injured (even to the point of death), all the animals in the animal kingdom respect his roar from at least a half mile radius. In conclusion, the commentator stated that as an injured lion returns to his feet and begins to roar, all the animals in the animal kingdom (including the snakes) flee from him up to a mile and a half distance. The commentator stated that the reason for the increased distance of respect for the lion's roar was because it was as all the animals knew that a lion that has been injured and healed is more dangerous than a lion that has never been injured. Just because someone has been injured or hurt emotionally, mentally or even physically, never under estimate the power of recovery—because there is power in hearing from the man with the scars!

The Apostle Paul was struck down on the road to Damascus where he became blind for three days. While I was reading the account of Paul's transformation, I began to be reminded of all the past sermons that I have heard preached from a traditional point of view where the preachers would always say that Paul was Saul before he got knocked off of his horse and fell to the ground blind. I do not find evidence that he was sitting on a horse. If he was, I would have to suggest the horse that he sat on was a "high horse" and not that of a four-legged animal. I would have to say that he fell from his high horse, holier than thou attitude that most religious people seem to have. Though he fell, he got up! He fell as Saul, but he got up a new man named Paul. He went from persecuting Christians to attacking religion talking about change. This guy had done an about-face-180 degree-turn-around.

Just because someone has been injured or hurt emotionally, mentally, or even physically, never under estimate the power of recovery!

Paul became the most prolific writer of the finished work of Calvary that later became two-thirds of the New Covenant. The New Covenant is what we now refer to as the New Testament. My life now is much like Paul's was then. Upon my transformation, there are those who talk terrible about and against me because of the things that I have done in my past. They do so much in the same way as the earlier Christians and the Jews did toward Paul after his conversion. Even the disciples stood at a distance not knowing if his conversion was real or not. They even discussed whether or not if they could trust him after all he had done as Saul. This is okay with me as it is unavoidable. Paul and I both have had terrible reputations that attempt to follow us into our new life of freedom. This is true of anyone whose past is all people have to go by.

The disciples represent our families and our friends, our bosses and even our church. They are all waiting to see if our change is real or not. I personally feel that real change is evident and can be seen by anyone, but the trust issue—well, that's the kick in the butt. Others need time to accept our change and trust is earned not given. This happens on its own as we remain consistent in our new life. As for myself, I know that there are those who sit on the sidelines watching and wondering if I am who I now say I am, and if this message of redemption that I now preach is real or not. All I can say is stick around to see for yourself.

How others perceive me, think about me, or even talk about me does not bother me anymore. I know who I am! When God gave me the title to this final chapter, "A Finished Work with Unfinished Business," I thought, "Well, this ought to come natural." As I have left unfinished business everywhere I have been, this always left me totally frustrated with myself and the feeling that I would never experience real satisfaction. It wasn't until I read what the Apostle Paul wrote in Acts 20:24 that I realized that there really is true satisfaction that comes from something remaining "unfinished."

Acts 20:24

"However, I consider my life worth nothing to me; my only aim is to finish the race and complete the task the Lord Jesus has given me—the task of testifying to the good news of God's grace." (NIV)

What the Apostle Paul is stating here is that he considered his life worth nothing "if only" or "if all" He did was come to a finish. His desire was not to finish testifying of the gospel of God's grace. Paul, as with myself, did not look to finish, but to continue testifying of the gospel of God's grace.

How others perceive me, think about me, or even talk about me does not bother me anymore. I know who I am!

Our destination is the beginning of a new life in a direct relationship with God.

Galatians 3:25:

"But now you have arrived at your destination: By faith in Christ you are in direct relationship with God." (MSG)

To be about the unfinished business of the finished work of redemption is to testify of the gospel of God's grace that has been shown unto you. It's called Christian service. Christian service is ministry and is what a mature Christian is to do. The more you grow, the more you will desire to help others. You move out of self-centeredness and become others-conscious.

When we experience change in a way that I have experienced change, you will not want to keep it to yourself. You will desire to help others through their pains of past mistakes and failures just as others had done for you. You will reach out your hand of help and say, "Take my hand and I will show you the way out of this hell that you are in."

Our testimonies are a combination of the words we speak and the lives we live. It's called "walking the talk," and this is only done by modeling and not by moralizing—not placing anyone above the other, but treating everyone equally. Just because others have gone before us, and there are those coming behind us, does not make anyone more than or less than the other.

Our testimonies are a combination of the words we speak and the lives we live. It's called "walking the talk," and this is only done by modeling and not by moralizing.

I can't help but to think how the children of Israel might have viewed each other. I wonder sometimes if the ones who passed through the Red Sea first reached back to help those who were following behind, or help those who may have stumbled and fell to get up. I would like to say yes, but I would possibly be correct to say that there were some who stepped over them as they were running from their enemies. I have also wondered how long it would take for a message to filter through four to six million people by word of mouth and the message to remain the truth.

In the wilderness, there were no cell phones, internet, or even a microphone. It was a "he said, she said" message relay system. I would imagine that with each person, they put their own twist to the message and by the time it reached those who were in the rear of the line, there was very little truth left in the message. It's like telling a fish story. Every time it is told, the lie grows bigger and bigger and the message gets away. It is for this reason that I have asked God to bring me back into the truth of His Word—the gospel of His grace.

My conclusion of the gospel (good news) of grace is that I am redeemed. I am the righteousness of God in Christ Jesus. I am a victor; I am an overcomer, not because I have overcome some things, but I have overcome them because that's who I am. The work of redemption has been fully completed in the bodily form of Jesus Christ, and we are that Body!

My conclusion of the gospel (good news) of grace is that I am redeemed. I am the righteousness of God in Christ Jesus.

This, my friend, is a message that is way too good to not share with others. Everyone deserves to know the truth of who they are. Everyone means everyone and not just other Christians, certain culture or ethnic groups, or circle of friends. Christ died for all! Just as Christ died for all, He also set all captives free. Although all are free there are still those who remain in captivity. They are still in bondage to an old lifestyle of sin because someone has forgotten to tell them that Jesus has set them free. They have not shared the message of redemption with them nor the reason and result of it.

I Timothy 2:4 (MSG)

"He wants not only us but everyone saved, you know, everyone to get to know the truth we've learned; that there's one God and only one, and one Priest-Mediator between God and us—Jesus, who offered himself in exchange for everyone held captive by sin, to set them all free. Eventually, the news is going to get out. This and this only has been my appointed work; getting this news to those who have never heard of God, and explaining how it works by simple faith and plain truth." (MSG)

To be about the unfinished business of the finished work of redemption is to testify of the gospel of God's grace that has been shown unto you.

The message of redemption really is simple, yet profound. Christ was crucified, died, buried, resurrected, quickened, and seated on the right hand of God. When we come to realize that this redemptive work was also done in us, His victory over death and hell becomes our victory, and we become free from our sins in the very moment that we choose to believe it to be true. Although each day is packed with decisions to be made, there is but one decision to make to set yourself free. That is the decision to believe. A true revelation of redemption will absolutely set you free and you won't be able to keep your mouth shut about it. It is too good to keep to yourself! The Apostle Paul couldn't even keep quiet about it after he received the revelation of redemption. He even preached the message while he was imprisoned for preaching the message. I love the way the message/remix words Paul's response to King Agrippa in Acts 26:19-20:

> "What could I do, King Agrippa? I couldn't just walk away from a vision like that! I became an obedient believer on the spot. I started preaching this life-change—this radical turn top God and everything it meant in everyday life..." (MSG)

Paul went on to say that the reason he was arrested by the Jews (religious leaders) was because they wanted to keep God to themselves. The entirety of this book hinges on the message of redemption and has ever changed my life. I have now given it to you. In the movie, "The Life of Pi," Pi told of His story of redemption (so to speak) to a writer who wanted to publish it. The writer spoke and said, "So the story has a happy ending?" Pi responded saying, "I don't know, you tell me, as the story is now yours to tell."

I close with the lyrics to my personal favorite song, "Redeemed" by the artist, Big Daddy Weave. It was what inspired me to write this book.

"Redeemed"

Seems like all I could see was the struggle
Haunted by the ghosts that live in my past—
Bound up in shackles of all my failures
Wondering how long this is gonna last.
Then you looked at this prisoner and said to me,"Son,
Stop fighting a fight—it's already been won."

I am redeemed, you set me free.
So I'll shake off these heavy chains, wipe away every stain,
Now I'm not who I used to be.
I am redeemed, I'm redeemed."

All my life, I have been called unworthy,
Named by the voice of my shame and regret,
But when I hear your whisper, "Child lift up your head,"
I remember, Oh God, you're not done with me yet.

I am redeemed, you set me free.
So I'll shake off these heavy chains, wipe away every stain,
Now I'm not who I used to be.
I am redeemed, I'm redeemed."

Because I don't have to be the old man inside of me.
Because His day is long dead and gone
Because I have a new name, a new life, I'm not the same
And a hope that will carry me home.

I am redeemed, you set me free.
So I'll shake off these heavy chains, wipe away every stain,

Now I'm not who I used to be.
I am redeemed, I'm redeemed."

"I am redeemed!"

You also are the redeemed of the Lord when you choose to believe.

The choice is yours.

Kingdom Life Publishing

Kenneth Meadors
5 Jones Mill PL
Cartersville, GA 30120

docwkm@aol.com

Made in the USA
Lexington, KY
29 April 2017